The Merry Gentleman

A Musical

Book and lyrics by
Dorothy Reynolds and
Julian Slade

Music by Julian Slade

Samuel French – London
New York – Sydney – Toronto – Hollywood

CHARACTERS

Father Christmas
Aunt Mabel
Henrietta, her niece and god-daughter
Alison, Henrietta's first cousin, twice removed
Mr Ough, Henrietta's father
Burgess, a friend of the family, thought of as Cousin
Uncle Charles, distantly related to Mabel
Violet, Mabel's maid
Abel
Disabel } her two dumb waiters
Edward, a newcomer
Edith
Dora
Biddie
Rosie } Cousins
Sidney
Eustace
Rudolf
Rufus } two Reindeer
Snowman

ACT I   Mabel's drawing-room and the roof-tops.
              Christmas Night
ACT II   Christmasland
ACT III Mabel's drawing-room

Time—1910

THE MERRY GENTLEMAN

First performed at the Theatre Royal, Bristol, on December 24th, 1953, with the following cast:

Aunt Mabel	Dorothy Reynolds
Violet, her maid	Pat Heywood
Abel \\ two dumb waiters	Bob Harris
Disabel /	Alan Dobie
Cousin Margot	Barbara Leigh-Hunt
Cousin Rosie	Gillian Lewis
Cousin Thelma	Pat Routledge
Biddy	Lesley Nunnerley
Cousin Jack	Roy Skelton
Cousin Wally	Patrick Horgan
Burgess	John Warner
Alison	Joan Plowright
Edward	Donal Harron
Henrietta	Jan Wenham
Mr Ough, her father	James Cairncross
Uncle Charles	Norman Rossington
Father Christmas	David Bird

Produced by **Lionel Harris**
Settings by **Tom Lingwood**

THE SONGS

ACT I

1	Candles At Christmastime	The Company
2	Let's Start The Party	The Company
3	A Face In A Photograph	Henrietta
4	The Umbrella Song	Burgess and Chorus
5	There's Only One Father Christmas	Charles, Edward and Father Christmas
6	A First Cousin	Alison and Chorus
7	The Clue From The Cracker	The Company
8	The Sleigh Song	The Company

ACT II

9	Don't Be Rude to a Reindeer	Rudolf and Rufus
10	Search	Father Christmas and the Company
11	Speak To Me Snowman	Henrietta and Snowman
12	Speak To Me Snowman (*reprise*)	Alison and Burgess
13	Poor Henrietta, Poor Alison	Henrietta and Alison
	A Face In a Photograph (*reprise*)	Henrietta
14	Try A Little Bit of Moonshine	Father Christmas, Mabel and Violet
15	Try A Little Bit of Moonshine (*reprise*)	Charles and Chorus
16	I'd Love To Be In Love With You	Henrietta and Edward
17	The Snowfall Waltz	

ACT III

17a	Try A Little Bit of Moonshine (*reprise*)	Charles and Cousins
18	The Merry Gentleman	Father Christmas and Company
19	Ough	Mabel and Mr Ough
20	The Umbrella Song (*reprise*)	Alison and Burgess
20a	The Clue From The Cracker (*reprise*)	Henrietta and Edward
21	It's The Thought That Matters	Cousins
22	Finale	The Company

The music for this play is available from Samuel French Ltd

THE MERRY GENTLEMAN

The Merry Gentleman opened on Christmas Eve, 1953, at the Theatre Royal, Bristol. Dorothy Reynolds and I had met eighteen months before as members of the Bristol Old Vic Company and had already collaborated on another Christmas show—*Christmas in King Street*—which several years later we turned into a musical for London called *Follow That Girl.*

In the first production of *The Merry Gentleman* we were fortunate in having having a distinguished cast. As well as such established players as Dorothy Reynolds herself, James Cairncross, David Bird, Jane Wenham and John Warner, the show presented such outstanding "newcomers" as Joan Plowright, Pat Heywood, Patricia Routledge, Barbara Leigh-Hunt and Alan Dobie. It was during the run of *The Merry Gentleman* that Dorothy Reynolds and I were asked by the Director of the Bristol Old Vic, Denis Carey, to write a summer show for the Company. This turned out to be *Salad Days* which in August 1954 was transferred to the Vaudeville Theatre, London, where it beat all existing records for a musical by running for five and a half years.

The Merry Gentleman was revived twice at Bristol, first at the Little Theatre in 1970 and then back at the Theatre Royal again in 1983.

The intention behind this show is to present as many of the aspects of Christmas as possible—warmth, nostalgia and at times magic or absurdity—or both! My hope is that some of these intentions are as relevant now as they appeared to us in 1953.

Julian Slade, 1985

ACT I*

A comfortable drawing-room, somewhere out of London, in the year 1910. Christmas Night

There is a large fireplace back C with two doors on either side of it, and exits into both wings. Off L is the hall, and off R a dining-room that has been cleared for supper and dancing. There is a minimum of furniture but just enough to make the room look cosy. It hardly needs more than a settee and one armchair (or possibly a large pouffe). Standing near the fireplace is a beautifully decorated Christmas tree, at the foot of which is a giant cracker. There are presents hung on the tree and piled up around it

When the CURTAIN rises, the stage is dark except for the glow of the fire. Unseen the Company is singing softly (pre-recorded)

During the song, Aunt Mabel enters with a lighted taper and lights the candles on the tree

Song 1: Candles At Christmastime

Company   Candles at Christmastime
We bring them out at Christmastime
We light them every year
And as the flames appear
We feel the joy and cheer
Of Christmastime.

When the snow is falling falling
And the elements fright you
The Christmas tree is calling calling
And the candles invite you.

Candles at Christmastime
We welcome them at Christmastime
They twinkle on the tree
As pretty as can be
The perfect sight to see
At Christmastime.

By the time the song is over the Lights are fully up. The music modulates into "Let's Start the Party" and is held behind the following:

Mabel (*humming*) "Good-evening—Good-evening" (*She notices the audience and speaks*) Oh, good-evening. I'm Aunt Mabel ... spinster ...

---

*N.B. Paragraph 3 on page ii of this Acting Edition regarding photocopying and video-recording should be carefully read.

of this parish. This is my tree, my fire, my house. And it's my party. I always give one, you know, every Christmas Night—for the young people in the family. Not strictly the family of course—they bring their friends. But it's usually the same lot. There's my god-daughter, Henrietta—most important. And her father—he's rather sweet. He's a widower. (*She smiles confidingly*) Then there's Uncle Charles—he always dresses up as Father Christmas. He loves doing it—it makes him feel so important. Only he can't come this year. He's got influenza. I think we shall manage without him—I've invited someone to take his place. Then there's Cousin Alison, Cousin Burgess—he's not really a cousin but we think of him as one—and perhaps half a dozen others—all very charming and very welcome—like yourselves. They seem to be arriving now. You'll excuse me, won't you?

Violet, a maid, and Abel and Disabel, two menservants, enter from one side with trays of drinks. Abel is young and bright, Disabel is exceedingly old and decrepit

From the other side, the Guests enter severally, during the following verse

Song 2: Let's Start The Party

Mabel **Servants** }	Good-evening
Cousins	Good-evening
Mabel **Servants** }	How are you?
Cousins	Quite well, thank you. How cosy and sweet It's so lovely to meet
Mabel **Servants** }	Is it cold outside?

Burgess, Alison and Edward enter

	Good-evening
Burgess **Alison** **Edward** }	Good-evening
Mabel **Servants** }	How are you?
Burgess **Alison** **Edward** }	Quite well, thank you.
Mabel **Servants** }	What will you drink?
Burgess **Alison** **Edward** }	Now just let me think It's so hard to decide.

Henrietta and Mr Ough enter

Mabel ⎞ **Servants** ⎠	Good-evening
Henrietta ⎞ **Mr Ough** ⎠	Good-evening.
Mabel ⎞ **Servants** ⎠	How are you?
Henrietta ⎞ **Mr Ough** ⎠	Quite well, thank you.
Mabel	What a charming dress!
Henrietta	It is old, I confess I have just had it dyed
1st Half	How are you?
2nd Half	How are you?
1st Half	How's Grandma? And Clara? And Sarah? Aunt Minnie? And Winnie? And Mister Smith's sister? (*Pause*) And Uncle Tom? (*Pause*)
2nd Half	Quite well thank you.
All (*solemnly*)	We are cousin, niece or brother Or the friend of someone's mother And we're polite to each other. (*Pause*)
1st Half	Good-evening
2nd Half	Good-evening
All	How are——

A rigid pause, then Henrietta and Alison exchange looks and break in

Henrietta	Excuse us, Aunt Mabel, If we interrupt
Alison	Forgive us, pray If what we say Seems a little abrupt
Henrietta	It's this— Couldn't we miss The conventionality?
Alison	And be Happy and free
Both	Without formality?
All	Let's start the party right away Today is Christmas Day And a Christmas party ought to be gay Let's start the party right away Let's dance and sing and play We are glad we've come, we're happy to stay! Parties should not Be too sedate Start them early And end them late

>   Let's start the party right away
>   Today is Christmas Day
>   And a Christmas party ought to be gay!

The song now becomes a "double" number. While the girls repeat the previous refrain, "Let's start the party ..." etc., all the men sing the following:

Men   Conversation too polite
                    Can continue half the night
                    We must not be dreary family bores
                    (We must not be dreary bores)
                    Let's forget the clothes we wear
                    Shiny shoes and tidy hair
                    Let's forget those dull society laws
                    (Let's forget those dull old laws)
>   Let's lose our dignity
>   And joy in letting it go! (Away with it!)
>   Our Christmas party comes
>   But once a year as you know (Make hay with it!)
                    Choose the way to have your fun
                    It's not the same for everyone
                    Do the things you've always wanted to do
                    (Do the things you want to do!)
All   Let's start the party
                    Right away! Right away!
                    Let's start the party right away!

Mabel and the Guests dance off R *towards the supper-room*

During the song, Abel and Disabel have been just sufficiently in evidence. While both are capable of joining in the sung choruses, neither ever speaks a word

> *After the general exit Abel and Violet clear a glass or two and exit smartly, possibly with a pinch and giggle on the way*

Disabel picks up a solitary glass and begins a long, long trail towards the exit

> *He is not half-way there when Burgess enters with his umbrella. Burgess looks about him, walks up and down, swaggers, and finally speaks to Disabel who is by now almost at the exit*

Burgess Will you ask Miss Henrietta if she will be good enough to have a word with me?

> *Disabel bows and totters off*

> *Abel enters. He is about to cross, but stays to watch Burgess with innocent fascination*

Burgess swaggers, smoothes his hair, lays hand to heart, embraces his umbrella with sudden passion and murmurs "I love you". He turns, sees Abel. Abel bows, relieves him of his umbrella and is about to go off with it

> (*Frenzied*) No, no, no, no, no! (*Retrieving it, he pants a little*) Thank you, I prefer to keep it.

Abel retires behind the tree but reappears at once covertly to watch Burgess who is now kneeling and passionately mouthing. The umbrella incommodes him. He lays it aside

Abel dodges away as Alison enters

Alison Burgess!
Burgess (*leaping up, dusting his knees and seizing the umbrella*) Oh, hullo Alison.
Alison Dear Burgess, had you fallen down?
Burgess No.
Alison (*tenderly*) Did you hurt yourself?
Burgess I hadn't fallen I tell you.
Alison Oh. Did you drop something?
Burgess No, thank you.
Alison (*hopeful*) Were you waiting for someone, perhaps?
Burgess As a matter of fact I was.

Alison comes closer

The most beautiful girl in all the world.

Alison blossoms

Alison Oh Burgess!
Burgess (*looking straight past her, off*) Oh Henrietta!
Alison (*sharp with disappointment*) Shall I take your umbrella and put it in the hall for you?
Burgess No, thank you. I like to have it. It gives me confidence.
Alison I wish I had something to give me confidence.
Burgess (*bored*) Do you?
Alison (*sighing*) Here's Henrietta.

Henrietta enters, carrying her handbag, followed by Abel, who goes behind the tree

Henrietta Burgess dear—oh Alison, how lovely you look in that dress!
Alison (*drifting away*) What's the use of looking lovely? It does me no good.

Alison exits

Henrietta Poor Alison! She always seems so sad these days.
Burgess Does she?
Henrietta You wanted to see me Burgess? Oh, no-one's relieved you of your umbrella. Let me——
Burgess No, no, no, it's all right. (*Gaily*) You can lose umbrellas that way, you know—leaving them in the hall. The umbrellas I've lost that way! Oh people don't mean to *steal* them, I realize that. It's just that they take them by mistake. And then where are you? You're without an umbrella! The money I've spent on umbrellas in a single year!
Henrietta Really? I'm sorry.
Burgess Oh it doesn't matter. I can well afford it.
Henrietta Yes, you're looking prosperous. We've hardly met since last Christmas, have we?

Burgess No, but I've thought of you, Henrietta.

Henrietta Have you?

Burgess I always do, but particularly this year because it's been rather a good one for me.

Henrietta I'm so glad.

Burgess Yes, I've been promoted. I'm Area Manager now.

Henrietta Congratulations! It sounds important.

Burgess It is rather. I have my own office now, and my own secretary, and my own telephone. Also I happen to have been elected President of the Golf Club. (*He swings his umbrella like a club*)

Henrietta Because of your game, I expect.

Burgess Oh yes. And the chaps like me, you know.

Henrietta I'm sure they do.

Burgess People do like me. I've discovered that. I don't know why it is. Being able to play the piano at parties—that sort of thing. Yes, all-in-all, a *very* good year. It's funny, I've known you ever since we were children, and I used to come and play in your garden . . .

Henrietta Yes. Dear Burgess, I've always thought of you as one of the family——

Burgess "Dear Burgess" you said! (*Fervently kneeling, incommoded by the umbrella*) Oh, but I'm *not* one of the family. I'm not related to you, dearest Henrietta!

Henrietta Burgess!

Burgess Darling Henrietta——(*He lays the umbrella aside*)

Henrietta Why are you kneeling down? Get up!

Burgess There's nothing in the world I'd like more than to be related to you!

Abel comes from behind the tree, takes the umbrella, hangs it on the mantelpiece, and retires

Henrietta How do you mean? I'll get Father to adopt you, if you like.

Burgess Oh not in that way you funny little thing! I mean Henrietta, will you——? (*He stops, abruptly suspicious, turns and sees his umbrella has gone*)

Henrietta What is it, Burgess? You were saying, you mean——?

Burgess (*his attention gone*) I-I-I-I-I m-m-m-m-ean——?

Henrietta What's the matter?

Burgess N-n-n-n-othing. I-I-I- (*hopelessly*)-I've lost my umbrella.

Henrietta Never mind that now. You were saying . . .?

Burgess I seem to be kneeling down. How ridic-ridic-ridic——

Henrietta Not at all. You were telling me about your promotion.

Burgess Oh that. (*He looks round wildly*) I shall never be able to hold that job down.

Henrietta Why ever not?

Burgess The fact is it's too b-b-b-b-big for me. I've had a terrible year. Sometimes I don't know whether I'm on my head or my-my-my-my——

Henrietta You'll be all right. And then there's the golf-club.

Burgess It's hopeless.

Henrietta Why?

Burgess They only elected me because I'm easy to p-p-push around. Nobody really likes me, you know. They're always saying things about me behind my back. I d-d-dread going there—you've no idea how awful it is—I-I-I——

Henrietta Oh look! There's your umbrella, hanging on the mantelpiece.

Burgess What? Oh so it is? (*He takes it, swings it laughing, and plays a golf stroke*) However did it get there?

Henrietta You were saying, Burgess . . .?

Burgess Was I? Oh yes. (*Loudly*) I was saying Henrietta, that I've had a remarkably good year.

Mabel sweeps in and seizes Burgess's umbrella

Mabel Burgess! Has no-one relieved you of your umbrella? I'm so sorry. Abel!

Abel appears

Take this.

Abel goes off

Henrietta stifles her laughter. Burgess looks a picture of misery

Mabel My dear, I do hope you're enjoying the party. You don't look as if you are.

Burgess Oh yes, th-th-thank you.

Mabel I want you to play the piano for us, you know.

Burgess Oh no, I've lost the ha-ha-ha-hang of it somehow, I-I-I——

Mabel Well go and say nice things to Cousin Alison for me. Look she's over there, looking so lonely and sad.

Burgess If you s-say so. Will you excu-cu-cu-cu——

The end of the word fails to come. He bows with tongue-tied rigidity to both of them and goes

Henrietta laughs

Mabel You mustn't laugh at him, Henrietta. Poor little man!

Henrietta It isn't that, I've just realized——

Mabel Realized what?

Henrietta He was trying to propose to me.

Mabel Oh dear! I hope I didn't interrupt.

Henrietta (*laughing*) No!

Mabel I suppose you've no thought of accepting him?

Henrietta Burgess? Oh no. I could never marry Burgess. And besides, the fact is—actually—there's someone else.

Mabel Henrietta!

Henrietta Yes. Oh Aunt Mabel, I've fallen so dreadfully in love.

Mabel My dearest child, I am delighted! Come and tell me all about it. (*She sits on the settee*)

Henrietta Oh thank you. (*She sits beside her*)

Mabel (*taking her hand*) Now—when did it happen?

Henrietta This morning.
Mabel Oh. It's all quite new.
Henrietta Yes.
Mabel What's his name?
Henrietta I don't know.
Mabel Oh. Where did you meet him?
Henrietta I've never met him.
Mabel You've never met him. You ... saw him somewhere?
Henrietta No, I've never seen him.
Mabel You've never seen him. Go on, dear.

Song 3: A Face in a Photograph

Henrietta

He's only a face in a photograph
A picture without any name
He's not very smart or superior
He can't even boast of a frame—
But when I first saw him he looked at me
As no-one had looked at me before
He's only a face in a photograph
But he is the man I adore.

Some girls think an earl would be heaven-sent
But I never aimed as high as that
My hero is just an advertisement
He's not even glossy—he is matt.

He's only a face in a photograph
But love isn't always so blind
And I knew the moment I looked at him
That this was the man I must find
For somehow his face has enchanted me
My heart's not my own any more
He's only a face in a photograph
But he is the man I adore.

Mabel Well dear, it all sounds most romantic.
Henrietta (*in a dream*) Oh yes!
Mabel Where did you come across this photograph?
Henrietta In my stocking.
Mabel More and more romantic. What was it doing there?
Henrietta It was—it was—oh Aunt Mabel, I think you'd better know *everything*.
Mabel I think I'd better.

Henrietta opens her handbag and takes out a bottle. This should be quite large and come very obviously from a chemist rather than a wine-merchant. Henrietta holds it up rapturously

Henrietta There!

Mabel Where? Forgive me if I'm stupid, but why are you waving that bottle of medicine at me? Are you ill?

Henrietta Perhaps I am, just a little. But this isn't a medicine. This is an elixir.

Mabel A what?

Henrietta A tonic.

Mabel But you don't need a tonic, do you? (*Aside*) I shall, in a minute.

Henrietta No, no. You don't understand. The photograph is *on* the bottle of tonic. I told you. He's an advertisement, you see. (*She hands her the bottle*)

Mabel (*faintly*) I see. (*She reads*) "The Secret of Perpetual Happiness. Take MOONSHINE, for outer shine and inner shine. MOONSHINE—the Amazing New Health-giving, Life-giving, Youth-giving Elixir, propounded, expounded and compounded by the One and Only DR BEAMISH. Available at all chemists, three shillings and twopence a bottle." (*She points to the picture*) Dr Beamish I presume?

Henrietta runs to her and looks over her shoulder

Henrietta (*ecstatic*) Yes! (*She reads*) "Are you Tired and Worried?"

Mabel nods

"Nervous and Irritable?"

Mabel nods again

"Feeling your Age?"

Mabel passes a limp hand down her face and pats under her chin

"Take MOONSHINE!"

Mabel is about to take a swig, then recollects herself

Mabel Am I to understand, dear, that you are in love with this Dr Beamish?

Henrietta Oh yes! Can't you see why?

Mabel Not quite. But I'll persevere. (*Peering*) He does seem to have nice eyes.

Henrietta And a *lovely* smile.

Mabel (*baring her teeth*) Yes, it is rather dazzling.

Henrietta And a noble, manly forehead.

Mabel M'm. What one can see of it. That hair ...

Henrietta What's the matter with his hair? It's beautiful hair. Dark—rich—luxuriant ...

Mabel There's certainly a lot of it. But it does rather obscure the view don't you think? What with the moustache, and the beard, quite apart from what's on top. Really dear, I may be missing something, but it seems to me you might just as well have fallen in love with a bear-skin rug.

Henrietta (*snatching the bottle*) Oh you're beastly! I might have known you wouldn't understand.

Mabel I did say he had nice eyes.

Henrietta You're going to tell me to forget about the whole thing, aren't you? But it's no use, because I can't.

Mabel No, I wasn't going to tell you to do that. But there's one question I'd like to ask you, Henrietta. Who do you think *put* Dr Beamish in your stocking?

Henrietta (*sulkily stuffing the bottle back into her bag*) Father Christmas, I suppose.

Mabel There's always a good reason behind everything Father Christmas does.

Henrietta (*surprised by the conviction in her voice*) How do you know?

Mabel Surely we all know that, don't we? So there's only one thing for you to do about your Dr Beamish.

Henrietta (*suspiciously*) What's that?

Mabel Find him.

Henrietta Oh, darling Aunt Mabel! (*Embracing her*) You are the best, most understanding godmother a girl ever had! I *will* find Dr Beamish! I *will*! I'll find him even if I have to go to the other ends of the earth!

Mabel Oh I hope you won't have to go as far as that.

Henrietta is about to run off

> *Mr Ough and Edward enter. Absorbed in what he is saying Mr Ough leads Edward across stage ignoring the two ladies*

Mr Ough ... so when the last war came along, I tried to explain to my poor old mother—she was a little deaf by then—"No, Mother" I said. "This war we are fighting is not the Crimea, dear. It's the Boer War." "A good cause" she said. "No-one should ever be allowed to become a bore." ... Ah, Mabel!

Henrietta (*aside to Mabel*) Don't tell him.

Mr Ough Don't tell me? Don't tell me what? Nobody ever tells me anything.

Henrietta (*kissing him*) You know that's not true, Father.

Mr Ough Henrietta, have you met—I'm sorry. I'm so bad at names.

Mabel Mr Edward Keene. This is my god-daughter, Henrietta.

Edward How do you do?

Henrietta How do you do, Mr Keene?

Mr Ough Lovely party as always, Mabel.

Henrietta Father, why don't you ask Aunt Mabel to dance?

Mr Ough Oh come, our dancing days are over.

Mabel raises an eyebrow

I'm sure your Aunt Mabel would rather sit down quietly and watch.

Henrietta Nonsense!

Mr Ough (*to Mabel laughing*) Dancing! At our age! Can you imagine it?

Mabel (*sweetly*) Just.

Mr Ough We don't know any of these modern things—all this rag-time and so on. In our day it was the Waltz—the Lancers—the Military Two-Step ...

Mabel The Minuet ...

Mr Ough Yes! No. Come now, Mabel, we don't go back as far as that.

Mabel Don't we? I was beginning to be afraid we did.

Henrietta Take her along Father, and don't talk so much.
Mr Ough What do you say Mabel? Will you accompany me to the other room?
Mabel I'll try and totter that far. (*She takes his arm*)
Mr Ough (*as they go*) I'm looking forward to this. It must be a hundred years since we took the floor together, Mary.
Mabel Mabel.
Mr Ough Of course. Mary was the name of my poor dear wife. Whatever can have put it into my head?
Mabel I can't imagine.

She exchanges looks with Henrietta as they exit

Henrietta (*laughing*) As you'll have gathered, my father is a bit vague.
Edward I'm afraid I'm just as bad. I didn't catch his name either.
Henrietta No. It's rather difficult to catch.
Edward Oh?
Henrietta In fact I doubt if anyone has ever caught it. It's spelt O—U—G—H.
Edward And how on earth is it pronounced?
Henrietta Father's never quite decided. It could be Ow, or Oo, or Uff ...
Edward Or Off—as in cough.
Henrietta Yes, I don't think we've ever thought of that one.
Edward It makes it difficult to know what to call you, Miss er——?
Henrietta Oh please call me Henrietta. We're all the family here and you mustn't feel out of it.
Edward Thank you Henrietta.
Henrietta And I shall call you Edward, if I may. Forgive me asking Edward, but why *are*—(*She checks herself*)
Edward Why *am* I here, you were going to say.
Henrietta Oh I don't think so. It sounds so rude.

Alison enters

Alison Henrietta, have you seen Burgess? I can't find him anywhere.
Henrietta I'm afraid not. Oh Alison, have you met Mr Keene?
Alison (*perfunctorily*) Good-evening. Burgess, Burgess!

Alison goes off as Burgess enters from the other side

Burgess Henrietta, have you s-s-s-een——
Henrietta Alison? She went that way.
Burgess No, no. I mean my um-um-um——
Henrietta Oh your umbrella. No, Burgess, I'm sorry. By the way, have you met Mr Keene?
Burgess (*sadly searching*) P-p-p-pleased to make your aqua-qua-qua-qua——

Burgess exits

Henrietta Two cousins.
Edward They seemed a bit worried.

Henrietta I'm afraid they weren't very polite. But please don't think you're not welcome Edward, because you are.

Edward It's nice of you to be so kind. But I don't expect to be treated as one of the family. I'm here in a professional capacity.

Henrietta Don't tell me you're a conjuror?

Edward No.

Henrietta A Punch-and-Judy Man?

Edward No. I'm a Father Christmas. Your aunt has engaged me to dress up as Father Christmas and give out the presents.

Henrietta Edward, how lovely!

Edward Yes, but is it? I gather you have an uncle or someone who always does it.

Henrietta Uncle Charles, only he's got influenza. We've always let him do it, you know, because he likes it, but really he has been getting a bit stale lately—and rather cross too. I'm sure you'll do it much better.

Edward I'm a little nervous. It's my first go at this.

Henrietta It's very easy. (*Looking at him*) But I must say, Edward, it does seem rather a curious job for a young man like you to be doing.

Edward Oh, I'll take any job that comes along. I'm a Younger Son, you see.

Henrietta Oh dear. You mean you're not quite respectable?

Edward Not at all respectable. Younger Sons never are. I wanted to be an engine-driver, but I went off the rails. I ran away to sea—I planted sugar canes—I've been a dustman, watchman, footman, rich man, poor man, beggar man——

Henrietta (*wide-eyed*) Not thief?

Edward Certainly. You name it, I've been it.

Henrietta Edward, how very romantic! And now you're a Father Christmas! Have you got a beautiful costume?

Edward Fairly beautiful. Will you tell me where to change?

Henrietta Of course. This way.

The doorbell rings

Oh there's the doorbell. Never mind. Someone will answer it.

She begins to lead Edward off, forgetting her bag, which she leaves on the settee

I'm sorry to have asked so many questions. But it *is* nice that you're here, and I'm awfully glad you're being paid for it. Come along.

As she takes him out through one of the upstage doors, the doorbell clangs loudly

Mr Ough enters from the supper-room meeting Burgess crossing agitatedly the other way, somewhat breathless

Burgess Uncle Arthur, have you s-seen my umbrella?

Mr Ough I expect Disabel put it in a safe place.

Burgess Well where *is* Disabel?

Mr Ough No idea.

The doorbell rings again

He should be answering the door.

He exits to the hall

Burgess (*calling*) Disabel! Disa—a—a—oh, this is desperate!

Burgess runs off

Mr Ough enters from the hall with Uncle Charles, who carries a small suitcase

Mr Ough Well Charles, I'm delighted you've come after all. Come to the fire. You look frozen.

Charles (*very thick with catarrh*) Couldn't get anyone to answer the door.

Mr Ough Well, well, you're here now. To tell you the truth, it's all a great surprise to me. I didn't know you *weren't* coming.

Charles (*indignantly*) I must say that's unaccountable, Arthur. My influenza has been noticeably bad this year. (*He takes a Father Christmas costume out of his case and holds the gown in front of the fire*) In fact I don't know if it's really wise—changing one's clothes—perhaps if I aired them a bit . . .

Mr Ough You can put them on in the little room up here. (*He points to the second upstage door*)

Charles (*testily*) Of course, of course. That's where I always change. I'll have to hurry. Presents at ten o'clock. There mustn't be a hitch.

Mr Ough Oh there'll be no hitch now you're here. Now, there was something I was *doing* when you arrived—something I was doing with Mabel—something rather disagreeable—what was it? I know. Dancing. Oh dear! (*He looks off and brightens*) Oh good, the music seems to have stopped. Better make myself scarce before it starts again. Cheerio Charles! See you on the Christmas tree!

Mr Ough exits

Charles looks sternly after him, then retires through the second upstage door, carrying his costume and suitcase

Burgess enters with Disabel, who carries a collection of umbrellas

Burgess It has to be my *own* umbrella, you see. Otherwise it's no g-g-good. (*He tries one after another and—after suitable business—finds his own*)

Song 4: The Umbrella Song

(*Singing*) Oh tell Henrietta
I'm feeling much better
Oh find her and tell her
I've got—my umbrellher!
It's madness, it's folly
To lose your umbrolly
For what is a fellow
Without—his umbrellow?

It's a wonderful healer
Just to hold an umbrealer
I am feeling quite well
Since I found my umbrell!
Oh tell Henrietta
I'm feeling much better
Oh find her and tell her
I've got—
My umbrellher—brolly—brellow—brealer
I've found my umbrell!

Disabel exits

If you're a man of substance and you want it widely
  known
You must carry an umbrella, for it gives a fellow tone
You can leave it in the office—
If you're sure it won't be lost—
For your colleagues to exclaim on it
And what it must have cost.
You can use it as a weapon if assaulted in the street
You can hide from any person that you do not wish to
  meet
You can stand and shake it, laughing, on the platform of a
  bus
You can whirl it—you can twirl it—
You can lean upon it—thus!

Cousins Eustace and Sidney now enter, both carrying umbrellas. Accompanying Eustace are Biddie and Rosie, while Sidney escorts Edith and Dora. Alison enters forlornly alone and watches from behind the tree

Burgess performs a lively acrobatic dance with his umbrella, while the others dancing more sedately behind him sing

Chorus   Oh tell Henrietta
He's feeling much better
Oh find her and tell her
He's got—his umbrellher!
It's madness, it's folly
To lose your umbrolly
For what is a fellow
Without—his umbrellow?
  It's a wonderful healer
  Just to hold an umbrealer
  He is feeling quite well
  Now he's found his umbrell!
Oh tell Henrietta
He's feeling much better
Oh find her and tell her
He's got—

His umbrellher—brolly—brellow—brealer—
He's found his umbrell!

General exit

Alison comes out from behind the tree, yearns after Burgess and follows

Charles enters, dressed as Father Christmas. He goes behind the tree, brings out a sack, takes a present and goes to hang it

As he disappears behind the tree Edward enters, also dressed up. He sees the sack, moves it, takes a present and disappears behind the tree

As he does so, Charles emerges the other way. Charles is surprised at the position of the sack, shrugs, takes a present and disappears as Edward reappears. Repeat ad lib. Finally they both come c together, reach for the sack, find an extra hand, raise their eyes and see each other. For a moment they think it is a reflection. Then Edward bursts out laughing

Edward Good heavens! It's Uncle Charles!

Charles (*exploding*) How dare you, sir? How dare you know who I am? Who are you?

Edward I'm Edward Keene.

Charles I'm no wiser. Who do you *think* you are? Getting yourself up—posing as Father Christmas—strutting round the tree as if you owned it! It's insufferable! I won't suffer it, you understand?

Edward I'm sorry, sir. I realize that by rights this is your part.

Charles Who told you? Mabel?

Edward You had influenza so she engaged me to take your place.

Charles Take my—engaged——(*Horror-struck*) You mean you're being *paid*?

Edward (*cheerfully*) In advance.

Charles This is too much. To do this to me! After years and years of loyalty.

Edward Well there you are. It's difficult. You've got the precedence and I've got the cheque.

Charles (*groaning*) Cheque! The vulgarity of it!

Edward Unfortunately I've cashed it. So you see I can't retire now—not honourably. Besides, I'm not sure that I want to. Henrietta——

Charles What has my niece got to do with this?

Edward She said she wanted me to feel I was part of the family.

Charles splutters

Look, Uncle Charles, why don't we settle this calmly over a drink?

Charles (*bursting*) I am *not* your Uncle Charles, and I do not drink!!!

Edward Pity. Well in that case, I can't, for the life of me, see what's to be done.

Song 5: There's Only One Father Christmas

At the start of this Edward is flippant and Charles extremely grumpy, but by the time they reach the refrain they forget their differences and think only of the figure they are representing

Edward	Two Father Christmases is one too many
	Rather than a glut of them, there'd better not be any
	It spoils the illusion—it makes the thing absurd—
Charles	You can't say "Father Christmases"—there's no such word!
Edward	You might say "Fathers Christmas"?
Charles	No, it simply wouldn't do.
	You might as well say "Santas Claus"—
Edward	And that is silly too.
Both	The name is in the singular, the plural is unknown
	And have you ever seen him when he hasn't been alone?
Edward	There's only one—
Charles	There's only one—
Both	Father Christmas!
	He's lived about a thousand winters through
Edward	With all the years he's seen
Charles	His sight is just as keen
Edward	His clothes are bright and clean
Both	And quite as good as new
Edward	He hasn't grown—
Charles	He hasn't grown—
Both	A wrinkle older!
	Since the day that Christmases began
	There's only one
	Father Christmas!
	An extremely well-preserved old man—
	He's well preserved.

To an um-ta rhythm they process round the tree and meet each other face-to-face again; Charles is by now enjoying himself and the situation

Both	It's the same in any language, whether English, French, or Dutch—
	Two Father Christmases is twice too much
Edward	If one of us is welcome, the other is *de trop*
Charles	There's only one solution—
Edward	But we both refuse to go.
Charles	The annual invitation which the family extend
	Has never once suggested that I should bring a friend
Edward	The pleasure of my company was bidden, it is true,
	But is the pleasure doubled, if I'm multiplied by two?

During the next refrain there is a subtle lighting change, and down the chimney comes a Boot, followed by a Large Form in scarlet and white which reveals itself as Father Christmas, in person. He stands monumentally behind them, watching them with contemptuous interest

Edward	There's only one—
Charles	There's only one—
Both	Father Christmas!
	Wherever there's a chimney he'll be there

With every roof in sight
He spends an active night
He's home before it's light
And shows no wear or tear.

Edward   He puts the gifts—
Charles   He puts the gifts—
Both   In every stocking
Without consulting any sort of plan
There's only one
Father Christmas
An extremely well-informed old man!
He's well-informed!

Father Christmas nods meaningfully. Charles and Edward, totally oblivious of what is behind them, now go into a "soft-boot" routine in which Father Christmas joins so that there are three Father Christmases doing identical steps. Father Christmas is still far enough upstage of them for them not to see him

Both   He hasn't grown
A wrinkle older
Since the day that Christmases began
There's only one
Father Christmas
An extremely well-preserved old man—
All   He's well preserved!

As Edward and Charles bring their heads together for the last harmonized notes, Father Christmas puts his between them so that they form a close picture for the end of the number. Edward and Charles slowly realize that there is a Third Person. They back away from him

Charles (*stuttering angrily*) This is too much! Twice too much! Some trick of Mabel's I suppose, some silly practical joke, some *game*! One interloper's bad enough——
Father Christmas SILENCE!!

The roar is so loud and resonant that all the lights flicker, and the fire goes in and out like a beating heart

Edward Yes. I thought it must be you.
Father Christmas Good. That's something. That's something, young man. Not everyone recognizes Christmas when they see him. (*He glares at Charles*)
Edward Why have you come?
Father Christmas You ask me why I'm come. Each of you, I take it, is supposed to be me. Me! Look at yourselves, and ask me why I've come!

Charles's gown is clutched round his middle. Edward's hat is awry

Look at yourselves, and then look at me. (*To Charles*) Do *I* have creases in my gown? Do I huddle it round my middle?

Charles I'm not——
Father Christmas SILENCE! (*To Edward*) Do *I* have a beard on a piece of elastic?

He pulls it and it snaps back. Edward winces

And do I have a miserable expression like that? (*Turning on Charles*) Or that? No, no, no, no, no! I am ALWAYS MERRY! (*He realizes he has not smiled once since his entrance. His voice turns to honey*) Always merry. A merry gentleman, that's what I am. And that's why I shall merrily turn you out of doors before you can do any more harm. I have work to do here, so begone! (*Waving a hand*) Avaunt, avaunt!
Edward You want us to go?
Father Christmas (*charmingly*) I want you to go.
Edward And where, if I may ask, do you want us to go?
Father Christmas (*wandering round the room*) The way I came, of course. Up the chimney.
Charles Up the——? I refuse.
Edward Ssh! And what then?
Father Christmas (*studying the tree*) You'll find out when you get to the top.
Charles But I can't go climbing chimneys at my age. Besides, it's not the kind of thing a man of my standing should do.
Father Christmas (*towering over him*) Your standing?
Charles Do you realize, sir, that I run Musty's Bank?
Father Christmas (*quietly terrible*) And do *you* realize, sir, that on this night of the year I run *you*—(*to Edward*)—and *you*—and everyone else in this house. So run along, both of you. Up the chimney with you.
Edward (*enjoying it all*) Come on, Uncle Charles! This is an adventure!
Charles I refuse. I absolutely refuse.
Father Christmas Be careful. Remember—I not only have the power to freeze your assets, but *you* as well.
Charles Freeze me? (*Unnerved*) But you'll burn me if I step over that fire.

Father Christmas does his Magic Gesture (hereafter recognizable as such) and the fire goes out

Edward You see, Uncle Charles? The circumstances are beyond our control. We'd better go.
Charles Very well. But I warn you—I shall take action. Drastic action. I shall write to *The Times*.

He exits up the chimney

Edward (*as he follows*) Will you do one thing for me?
Father Christmas What is it?
Edward Look after Henrietta.
Father Christmas I shall look after you all.

Edward waves and goes

Father Christmas toys with the presents on the tree and hums to himself

Mr Ough enters

Mr Ough Ah, there you are Charles. All togged up and ready for the fray, I see. Have you seen Mabel? I still haven't managed to finish that dance with her. I *say*, Charles, your costume is absolutely splendid this year. That padding is most convincing. You look positively bloated. Well done, well done! (*He pokes him hard in the tummy*)

Father Christmas doubles up

Mr Ough exits as Henrietta enters

Henrietta Edward! How lovely you look! Stand up straight though. Father Christmas may be old but there's no need for him to be doubled up. (*She pulls him up*) Oh yes, Edward. It's a wonderful make-up. You look so *ravaged* and *wrinkled*. But the beard's crooked. Here! (*She takes hold of his beard and pulls it sharply*)

Father Christmas Ow!

Henrietta (*laughing*) Oh Edward, I'm so sorry. You've stuck it. I thought it was on a piece of elastic. Now *where* is my bag? (*She sees it*) Ah, there it is. Thank goodness. I think I should die if I lost that.

Henrietta exits

Father Christmas rubs his chin and his tummy. Mabel's voice is heard, off

Mabel (*off*) Of course, dear, I'll put it on the tree for you.

She enters briskly with a small present

Father Christmas, fearing another assault, protects himself with a defensive gesture

Father Christmas No, no! Don't touch me!

Mabel stops dead in her tracks, stunned. The present falls from her hands

Mabel I wouldn't dream of it, Your Grace, Eminence, Worship, Majesty— Sir! (*On the last word she sinks into the deepest possible court curtsy*) Delighted and honoured.

Father Christmas You recognized me.

Mabel Of course.

Father Christmas You're the hostess? (*He helps her up*)

Mabel Yes. I thought perhaps you might recognize *me*.

Father Christmas Should I?

Mabel I was your pupil once.

Father Christmas What?

Mabel I trained at your place. Of course I was very young then ...

Father Christmas Oh, you mean a long time ago. The years pass and memory fades ... perhaps there is something familiar ...

Mabel I'm Mabel.

Father Christmas (*striking his forehead*) You're Mabel! Of course! Funny fat little Mabel you were then. Now let me see—what were we training you to be? A witch?

Mabel (*restraining herself, out of respect*) No ... o ... A Fairy Godmother. Possibly you've met my god-daughter, Henrietta?

Father Christmas A very pretty girl with a very large handbag?

Mabel That would be her. Charming, isn't she?

Father Christmas Charming. She pulled my beard.

Mabel How very unlike her! She has such nice manners usually. (*Tutting, she picks up the present and moves to the tree*) Really, the young people these days . . .

Father Christmas You're doing the tree. May I help?

Mabel (*immensely flattered*) Oh . . . well . . .

Father Christmas (*reading labels*) "Alison" . . . "Burgess" . . . Relatives?

Mabel Oh yes, they all are, except that rather sweet boy, Edward. I wonder where he is, by the way.

Father Christmas Up the chimney.

Mabel Oh.

Father Christmas Also a grumpy gentleman called Charles.

Mabel So he came after all?

Father Christmas Came—(*he gestures to the chimney*)—and went.

Mabel That's why the fire's out. I thought it was a bit chilly.

Father Christmas We can soon light it again.

Mabel Quite easily. I'll ring for Abel.

Father Christmas No need for that. (*He is about to do his Magic Gesture, then stops himself*) I'm so sorry. Perhaps you'd like to do it.

Mabel Oh no please, you.

Father Christmas It's your house. I think it should be you.

Mabel No, no, I simply couldn't in front of you. I'm terribly rusty and I'd be so ashamed if it didn't work.

Father Christmas Oh come on!

Mabel Oh all right then! (*Making a tremendous effort, she gestures at the fire and it lights*)

Father Christmas There! You haven't lost your touch. We should make a remarkable combination.

Mabel What do you mean?

Father Christmas You surely didn't think I came to your party just for fun?

Mabel People sometimes do. But I felt there must be a reason.

Father Christmas Christmas Eve is my night really, but every seven years I work overtime. I choose a family and then, on Christmas night, I drop in at their party and *do* something for them all.

Mabel How do you pick the family?

Father Christmas I let Rodney do it.

Mabel Rodney?

Father Christmas My head Reindeer. It used to be Rufus or Rudolf but they've retired.

Mabel How sweet of Rodney to choose *us*!

Father Christmas Pure accident. He simply shuts his eyes and puts a hoof on my chimney map. Lucky choice, though. This time *you* can help me.

Mabel I'd love to help. What would you like us to do for them all?

Father Christmas Don't exhaust yourself. The magic doesn't come yet.

Mabel relaxes

Now I suppose there's something they all want?

Mabel Oh yes! Now let me see, Alison wants a new evening shawl, and Edith wants bathsalts, and Eustace wants treacle toffee——

Father Christmas Not *things*, woman!

Mabel But I thought one always got things at Christmas.

Father Christmas These are just symbols—trivial knick-knacks—irrelevant—unimportant——

Mabel But rather pleasant, surely?

Father Christmas (*exploding*) It's all got completely out of hand! Once upon a time Christmas was Christmas, but now it's nothing but an orgy of commercial clap-trap! Wherever I look I see abominable travesties of Me dispensing junk like so many travelling salesmen! But when the real Father Christmas comes he brings real gifts.

Mabel (*a little bewildered*) Well I must say I hate cheap imitations——

Father Christmas For their *lives*, Mabel. Gifts for their *lives*.

Mabel Oh you mean Insurance Policies . . .

Father Christmas Try not to be obtuse. Now listen. You're none of you really happy, are you?

Mabel (*surprised*) Aren't we?

Father Christmas Take the girl with the handbag . . .

Mabel Henrietta?

Father Christmas She's looking for something, isn't she?

Mabel Yes, she is. How did you know?

Father Christmas Aren't you *all* looking for something? (*Pointing*) That girl over there . . .

Mabel (*looking off*) Yes—Alison . . .

Father Christmas Don't tell me she's happy! She has that hungry, *questing* look stamped all over her face.

Mabel Perhaps she hasn't had any supper.

Father Christmas She's coming this way. Let's watch her, and then—if you put your mind to it, Mabel—you may see what I mean.

They hide behind the tree

Music. Alison runs on in distress, followed by Edith, Dora, Biddie and Rosie

Song 6: A First Cousin

Girls	Alison! Alison!
	Won't you tell us what's the matter?
	Are you tired of the party chatter?
Alison	Oh my dears! Pity me!
	My first cousin Henrietta
	Always seems to manage better
	She's the one he loves
	I'm the one he merely shoves
	In affairs of the heart

> I am beaten at the start
> I'm a first cousin twice-removed
> I'm most unlucky with men
> Twice I've been removed from love
> It must not happen again
> I must not fail my third attempt
> To win my man's approval
> I'm a first cousin twice-removed
> And I don't want a third removal.
>
> My first removal was in eighteen-ninety-nine
> I loved a gentleman—I thought him quite divine—
> But he loved Henrietta so I said "Oh what's the use!"
> And removed myself to Manchester to live as a recluse.
>
> At length I reappeared, until in nineteen-seven
> I loved a gentleman—I thought him perfect heaven—
> But he loved Henrietta, so in sorrow and dispair
> I removed myself to Bromley with intent to perish there.

Girls   But you didn't?
Alison   No. I didn't.

> And now the love of my life emerges
> A passion that's full of romantic urges
> Sometimes I feel it almost verges
> On insanity! But it purges.

Girls   Who is it?
Alison   Burgess!

During the last refrain the Girls hum a sympathetic counterpoint

> I'm a first cousin twice-removed
> But my removals are through
> Here I am and here I stay
> For here is my Waterloo
> I'll cling to Burgess like a vine
> And melt his disapproval
> I'm a first cousin twice-removed
> But I won't have a third removal.
> Burgess!

Girls   Look out Burgess!
Alison   Here I come!

Alison exits, the Girls following

Father Christmas and Mabel emerge

Mabel Poor Alison! You were right. She certainly is looking for something.
Father Christmas And I can help her to find the way.
Mabel (*understanding at last*) I see! It's to be a search. A search for the thing they really want.

Father Christmas Something like that.

Mabel Lovely! Where do they begin?

Father Christmas Ah! This is where you come in. I usually start them off with a party game. Had you anything planned for this evening?

Mabel Well now, let me think. We had toyed with the idea of "Murder" . . .

He gives her a look

Hardly suitable perhaps?

Father Christmas Hardly.

Mabel "Sardines"?

Father Christmas "Sardines" can lead to many things but not necessarily to happiness.

Mabel Then, of course, there's the treasure-hunt . . .

Father Christmas That's it. The very thing! (*Slapping her on the back*) Mabel, you're a brick!

Mabel (*overcome*) Oh . . . Oh I'm so glad.

Father Christmas Perfect! What form was the treasure-hunt to take?

Mabel First I give each person a written clue like "Look in the bathroom cupboard" or "Ask Violet where the cat sleeps"—then this will take them on to the next clue, and the next, and so on and so on, until in the end——

Father Christmas They find their prize. But only if they work for it.

Mabel Exactly!

Father Christmas And the prize?

Mabel Oh, lollipops and that kind of thing.

Father Christmas But *this* time, Mabel, the prize will be——

Mabel (*excited*) Their happiness!

Father Christmas Instead of the lollipops.

Mabel Wonderful!

Father Christmas Let's get going. Where are the clues?

Mabel Abel has the bag of leading clues. A——

Abel suddenly appears with a bag of clues on a salver

Father Christmas Good-evening Abel.

Abel bows low

And the other clues?

Mabel Scattered all over the house, I'm afraid.

Father Christmas I don't think so. (*He snaps his fingers*)

Disabel totters on with another bag of clues on another salver

Good-evening, Disabel.

Mabel I do believe you know them!

Father Christmas Oh yes, they're both mine. (*He pats Disabel*) He's been with me three hundred years.

Mabel I thought when I hired them for the party there was something odd about them. Of course! You *sent* them! So you must have known who I was all the time. Funny fat little Mabel, indeed! You naughty old man, you've prearranged everything, haven't you?

Father Christmas Not quite everything. I didn't know about your treasure-hunt you see. So the clues have to be changed.

Mabel (*dismayed*) Oh but that's impossible! You've no idea how long it took me to write all those clues.

Father Christmas You really are being remarkably slow this evening, Mabel. And you were once such a bright little fairy. (*He gets into position for his Magic Gesture*)

Clues, clues, do as I say!
Help the seekers to find the way.

Music 6A. Both bags of clues flash (or jump)

There! (*He smiles smugly at Mabel*)

Mabel I'm sorry. It never occurred to me ... I lead such a humdrum life these days.

Father Christmas Now—for the leading clues, we must find—(*relishing the words*) a Suitable Receptacle.

Mabel Can't we just hand them round?

Father Christmas Mabel! Please! Let us try to use what little imagination we have left. (*His eyes roam the room and light on the giant cracker at the foot of the tree*) Aha! That's the place for them.

Mabel Oh but you can't undo that! I've made it so care—oh, of course ... I do beg your pardon ...

Father Christmas   Ticker-Tacker, Ticker-Tacker
Hop it, Clues, into the Cracker.

Music 6B. The bag vanishes from Abel's salver

Mabel You're wonderful!

The telephone rings

Excuse me ... (*She goes to the chimney and takes out an Edwardian-style telephone receiver*) Hello ... Very well, I'll tell him. (*She puts back the receiver*) That was Rodney. The sleigh's waiting.

Father Christmas We must waste no time. Now, we need a wand. Have you one handy?

Mabel There's one in my old green handbag I think. But where's that?

Violet enters with a handbag

Violet Your old green handbag, madam.

Mabel Violet! You clever girl. Was it magic, or did you just guess?

Violet It came to me, madam.

Mabel The handbag?

Violet It just came together in my hands.

Mabel Well, you are getting along nicely. Now I'll introduce you to a Very Important Person.

Violet (*curtsying*) Father Christmas, madam.

Mabel There. She knew.

Father Christmas And who is this clever little girl?

Mabel Violet. She's training to be Ultra-Violet, one of our future fairy godmothers.

Father Christmas (*to Violet*) Come up and see me sometime. I can give you
some useful introductions.
Mabel Isn't that kind? Now run along Violet. We've got work to do. And
put your cap straight, dear, or you'll never be Ultra.

Violet exits

Mabels takes a wand like a folded ruler out of her bag

Father Christmas So! We stand over the cracker ...
Mabel One on each side?
Father Christmas That's right. Ready? Now!

Mabel waves her wand and it collapses

Mabel Oh dear, I was afraid it would be self-conscious with you here.

*Father Christmas gives her a severe look and takes the wand. He waves it
majestically. Music 6C*

Father Christmas   Wand Wave, Cracker Flame,
                           Magic Work, Begin the Game.

The Lights change. Smoke begins to rise from the cracker

Mabel (*clapping her hands*) Look, it's working!
Father Christmas Of course.
Mabel Abel, call them all in. Quickly!

Abel runs off

Isn't this exciting?
Father Christmas This is the easy part. Just the beginning. Now it's up to all
of *them*.

Song 7: The Clue From the Cracker

During the first verse the Guests enter severally from L *and* R

Father Christmas ⎫	Would you like to play a game?
Mabel ⎭	You'll know it by its name
	It's a treasure-hunt
	And there's a prize
	You will have to use your eyes
All	We will have to use our eyes!
Father Christmas ⎫	The clue is in the cracker
Mabel ⎭	That is just the first one
	Hunt the second third and fourth
	The last one is the worst one
	This we give you freely
	The others you must find
	Look into things and over things
	Beneath them and behind.
All	Look into things and over things
	Beneath them and behind.

Father Christmas	There's a name on every clue
Mabel	A special one for you
	Pick your own clue
	Each has his own
	For you have to hunt alone
All	For we have to hunt alone.

The Lights and atmosphere change with the music. The fire goes out. The cracker is pulled. The Guests find their clues and take them unopened to their positions. From now on, each is, in effect, singing "alone". The tone is of wondering elation

Girls	The clue from the cracker is meant for me only
	I must follow in solitude, will it seem lonely?
	I must read it in secret and hide it away
	"Ask Father Christmas the way to the sleigh".
Men	The clue from the cracker I must not reveal it
	My eyes must be guarded before I unseal it
	No glance nor no gesture must give me away
	"Ask Father Christmas the way to the sleigh".
All	The others are cautious, I must not be bolder
	Be certain that no-one looks over my shoulder
	No friend or beloved persuade me to say
	"Ask Father Christmas the way to the sleigh."

As Alison quietly begins to sing the following the Guests go one by one to Father Christmas and then off up the chimney

Finally only Alison and Henrietta are left, with Father Christmas and Mabel shadowy figures in the background

Alison	How strangely changed
	The evening seems
	As though this search
	Might end my dreams
	And guide me by
	Some secret way
	To the joy I long for
	Night and day.

Henrietta now repeats this refrain with her, but singing a counter-melody. They stand in separate pools of light

Henrietta	
Alison	} How strangely changed ... *etc.*

With just enough music to allow time for Henrietta, Alison, Aunt Mabel and Father Christmas to exit up the chimney, the room begins to disappear and the scene "transforms" to the roof-tops

Father Christmas is at the reins of an enormous sleigh, with the whole Company (except Charles and Edward) banked behind him

Song 8: The Sleigh Song

All   We're galloping prettily over the city, we
Scorn to be drawn on the ground
We're out on the tiles and cover the miles
With patter and clatter of sound
Our rollicking rouses the attics of houses
Where people are sleeping in bed
They waken and wonder if they can be under
A thunder that roars overhead
A thunder that roars overhead.
    The hoppity-clop of the hoofs on the roofs
    And the speed of the steed and the sway of the sleigh
    Resound in the street with a regular beat
    And we sing as we swing on our way.
At a breath-taking pace we'll be flying through space
And be counting the mountains below
Oh if you're a stranger you might think it dangerous
Seeing the speed that we who—a!
Seeing the speed that we go.

The following eight lines are sung conjointly with the first eight lines of the second refrain

    Stars are gleaming
    Spell-bound dreaming
    Snow-clouds drifting
    Parting lifting
    We unheeding onward speeding
    Smoothly riding, air-borne, gliding,
    Earth deriding
    On we go!

We're easily able to dodge every gable
And miss all the chimneys and spires
We never fall off and we scoff as we cough
At the smoke of the folk who have fires
We're happily driving and as for arriving
We're well in the spell of our guide
With none of us knowing the way we are going
We trust it is just for the ride
We trust it is just for the ride

And the bounding, resounding repeat of the feet
In the white of the night and the jingle and ring
Of the bells on the sleigh as it bears us away
As we glide as we slide as we sing!

Slower tempo now, but still with strong rhythm

Remarkably soon we'll be close to the moon
And be spying what's lying below
It's all so enthralling we feel we are falling
As fast as a shower of—who—a!
As fast as a shower of snow!

CURTAIN

ACT II

Christmasland

A sparkling snowscape. Various small fir-trees are dotted about. In one downstage corner can be seen part of Father Christmas' Winter Palace. There is a practical entrance door, flanked by the heads of two Reindeer. (These should be made in such a way that the faces of Rudolf and Rufus can appear, to sing their song unimpeded.) Upstage, with his back to us, is a Snowman, complete with hat and pipe, immobile. "Sleigh Song" music

Charles enters, dragging a miniature sleigh. On it sits Edward, very relaxed and comfortable

Charles Where on earth are we?

Edward Not on earth at all. This is Christmasland! Pretty isn't it, Uncle Charles?

Charles (*stomping along*) I'm cold and I'm not your uncle and what I think I'm doing dragging *you* about the place I don't know! Get off you young oaf! (*He drops the reins*) The whole party's been a complete frost. First that filthy chimney and then a perfectly ghastly ride——

Edward What can you expect of a chartered sleigh? The others were lucky. They travelled comfortably in the jumbo.

Charles We were mad to entrust ourselves to those mangy old reindeer. You could see by their eyes they were deceitful beasts.

Rudolf I beg your pardon?

Charles I said "You could see by their eyes they were deceitful beasts."

Edward Yes, I heard you the first time.

Charles Then why did you beg my pardon?

Edward I didn't.

Charles You most certainly did. (*Mimicking*) "I beg your pardon" you said.

Rudolf If that is supposed to be an imitation of me it is tasteless and inaccurate.

Edward (*laughing*) Good heavens! It's the reindeer!

Charles What, those? (*He crosses over to look*) They can't have brought us here. Those are just heads on a wall. And pretty poor specimens at that.

Edward I expect they were let out specially for us—because we're second-class. Now they're back in retirement again.

Rufus (*straight into Charles's ear*) And there's no need to be rude to us just because of that.

Charles jumps back

Rudolf *You'll* be retiring, before long.

Rufus And then you'll be like us.

Charles What? Me? How dare you, sir! I am the Head of Musty's Bank!

Rudolf (*sniggering*) And soon *you'll* be just a Head on a Wall, won't he Rufus?

Rufus Undoubtedly, Rudolf.

Rudolf So kindly show a little respect.

Song 9: Don't Be Rude to a Reindeer

Rudolf ⎫ **Rufus** ⎭	Don't be rude to a reindeer When he's just a head on a wall He is at a disadvantage, for He can't kick back at all Hitting at a Chap who's weak and hoofless Is a cowardly thing to do You must never be rude to a reindeer When he can't be rude to you!
Rudolf	Ex-champions of the sleigh team Should preserve a princely pose
Rufus	So please don't tweak our whiskers Or plant kisses on our nose
Both	Personal re— Personal re— Marks are most unwelcome More especially if they're true
Rudolf	You must never be rude to a reindeer—
Rufus	He is such a very proud urbane deer—
Both	No, never be rude to a reindeer When he can't be rude to you.

During the "link" music the two men perambulate, Edward gaily, Charles crossly, while the Reindeers' heads nod from side to side

	Don't be rude to a reindeer It degrades him to appear
Rufus	With his antlers used as a hatstand—
Rudolf	And a dog-lead over one ear
Both	Polishing a Reindeer's nose with a duster Wounds his vanity through and through You must never be rude to a reindeer When he can't be rude to you!
Rudolf	To be put to bed in a dust-sheet Is enough to rouse one's wrath
Rufus	But it's even more insulting to be Sprayed with anti-moth
Both	Cleaning up a Reindeer's face with a clothes-brush Hurts his skin and feelings too

Rufus	You must never be rude to a reindeer
Rudolf	He can't bear to look a daft, inane deer—
Both	No, never be rude to a reindeer
	When he can't be rude to you!

After the song, Charles suddenly becomes petrified

Charles Listen.

Sleigh-bells and voices off

Edward It's them!
Charles It's Him! Quick, hide!

He seizes Edward and drags him behind a tree

Edward But Henrietta——
Charles Sssh!

Father Christmas, Mabel and the Sleigh Party enter. They are now in glamorous outdoor winter costume, with muffs, boots, fur hats etc.

Father Christmas Well Mabel, here we are!
Mabel Oh and it's all exactly as I remember it! I'm so excited I should like to clap on my wings at once and fly into the air. (*She does a gay pirouette*) Well darlings, what do you think of Christmasland?

Murmurs of wonder and approval

Henrietta It's beautiful.
Mabel And how do you all like your new clothes?

Delighted astonishment. Cries of "How extraordinary!" "Look at me" etc.

Mr Ough I don't remember changing.
Henrietta (*to Father Christmas*) Did you do this? How clever you are!
Father Christmas It was your aunt, actually.
Henrietta Aunt Mabel!
Mabel Oh it was nothing. I ran them up in no time.
Father Christmas We couldn't have you all catching cold.
Alison Oh Henrietta, yours is truly lovely.
Burgess Yes it *is*.
Henrietta I think yours is just as pretty, Alison.
Burgess *Do* you?
Henrietta Thank you, Aunt Mabel! (*To Father Christmas*) And thank *you* for bringing us here. I'd like to stay here always.
Father Christmas It's very dull in the off-season.
Mr Ough It reminds me of a honeymoon I once had in—what was the name of that snowy place, dear?
Henrietta Switzerland, Father.
Burgess Is it my imagination or is it rather cold? My hands are like ice.
Alison Take my muff, Burgess.
Burgess Oh no, I couldn't really. (*He takes it*)
Mabel I simply must have a peep at the old haunts. (*To Father Christmas*) May I consider myself at home?

Father Christmas Of course. But Mabel—(*sotto voce*)—don't forget we have work to do.

Mabel No, no, I won't. Violet, come with me.

Violet Oh yes madam.

Mabel knocks on the door of the Palace

  It is opened by Disabel

Mabel Oh, you got here ahead of us. Pretty nippy, weren't you? Isn't it wonderful to be back?

  She goes into the Palace with Violet. Disabel skips with delight and follows

Henrietta He must *belong* here.

Alison But why are we here?

Father Christmas Why? Don't you remember how it all began? This is a Treasure Hunt, not a pleasure trip. If you dawdle about idly, you will fre-e-e-eze!

All shiver and shake

  But if you hunt hard and diligently a special prize will be yours. In Christmasland, opportunity is in the air! Listen!

During the following song, Edward and Charles, behind the fir tree, pop their heads out from time to time and join in the song

Song 10: Search

(*Singing*)	These are your instructions which I beg of you to heed
	Clues are hidden round you and they all directly lead
	To what will make you happy, to the thing you feel you need
	So search! Search! Search!
Chorus	Let's make a start
	With hope in our heart
	And all play a part
	In the search!
	Where are the clues?
	There's too much to lose
	If we should refuse
	To search, search, search, search
	Look between the trees and up the hill and down the lane
	And if we seem defeated we will start the search again
	Where shall we go?
	We'll delve in the snow
	Above and below
	We'll search, search, search,
	Above and below
	We'll search!

Father Christmas	If you wander lazily or if you take your ease
	If you cease to circulate, your blood begins to freeze
	Stir and look around you and be active if you please
	And search! Search! Search!
Chorus	Do as we're told
	He's wise and he's old
	He bids us be bold
	And search!
	What's in his mind?
	Or what shall we find?
	Oh what lies behind
	The search, search, search, search
	Scatter round the house and over all the snowy land
	Will the thing we look for be discovered close at hand?
	Follow our friend
	It's just round the bend
	Or right at the end
	Of the search, search, search
	It's right at the end
	Of the search . . . search . . . search . . . search . . . *etc.*

All exit, marching and searching, except Father Christmas

Father Christmas (*to Edward and Charles behind the fir tree*) Now then, you two! I know you're behind that tree. Come out! (*Bellowing*) Come out! (*Cooing*) Come out. Daddy Christmas won't hurt you.

They come out, Edward nonchalant, Charles trembling with fear

Did you hear what I was saying to the others?
Charles Y-y-yes.
Edward We could hardly avoid hearing it.
Father Christmas Off you go then, and search.
Edward Don't worry. I will.
Father Christmas You seem very certain of what you want, young man.
Edward I should say so, and if you think there's a chance of my getting her, I'll search for as many of your old clues as you like.
Father Christmas That's the spirit.
Edward When do I get my smart new winter suit, like the other fellows?
Father Christmas When you've shown me you mean what you say.
Edward I mean it all right. Henrietta! Henrietta!

Edward exits

Father Christmas Now then, you. What about you?
Charles It's ridiculous to play at treasure-hunting at my age.
Father Christmas What has age got to do with it? It's Christmas. And I warn you, my lad, if you sit down and refu-u-use, you'll free-ee-eeze.

Charles leaps up in terror

Come to think of it you look rather cold at the moment. We'll go for a little ride. (*He gets into the small sleigh*)

Charles (*groaning*) Oh no! Not that again!

Father Christmas Remember what I said about freezing? Now ready—steady—Gee-up!

Charles gallops off with him unwillingly to music

Mabel enters in full fairy costume, complete with wings. Violet follows in a simpler costume, without wings

Mabel How do I look Violet?

Violet Oh beautiful, madam, you really do.

Mabel Arrange my wings for me. They seem to have shrunk since I last wore them. A little more to the left. No—not so far. You'll make me loop-the-loop. That's better. (*She does a dance step*) I wonder if I can still get on my points? (*She just manages it*)

Violet Oh madam, you *did* it! Wherever did you learn to do such clever things?

Mabel (*effervescent*) Here, Violet, here. It's the only place to come for fairy-teaching—like going to Paris to learn French.

She does a brilliant twirl. Violet watches her with breathless admiration

Violet Madam ...

Mabel (*dancing*) Yes Violet?

Violet Tell me honestly—do you really think I have the makings of a fairy?

She gets herself uncertainly into the "fifth position". Mabel stops dancing

Mabel Well now, let's have a look at you. (*She surveys her with a critical eye*) Yes ... there are possibilities ...

Violet wobbles

... a little hard to see at the moment, but they are definitely there. (*She taps her lightly with her wand*) I shall probably send you here when you're older.

Violet Oh madam!

Mabel If you're good, Violet, and work hard to be Ultra.

Father Christmas enters with Abel

And here's Abel. He's Father Christmas's assistant, aren't you Abel?

Father Christmas He's going to help plant the clues.

Mabel How nice. Why don't you take Violet with you? She'd love that, wouldn't you, Violet?

Violet Oh yes, madam!

Mabel Now Father Christmas and I have a lot to discuss, so fly away there's a good girl.

Violet (*giggling*) Oh madam, don't tease me! You know I can't fly yet.

Violet exits with Abel

Father Christmas and Mabel become very conspiratorial

Father Christmas Well, how do you think it's going?

Mabel Are they searching?

Father Christmas I think so. Except Uncle Charles. But I've *threatened* him.

Mabel Poor Uncle Charles! I don't think I've ever seen him smile.

Father Christmas (*grimly*) He'll smile by the time I've finished with him. As for the others, I thought we might follow them about, and possibly put a spoke in now and then.

Mabel But if they see us, won't that make them self-conscious—like my wand?

Father Christmas Well then, perhaps you could make yourself invisible.

Mabel That might be difficult too. I've got so used to being solid.

Father Christmas Have a try.

Mabel Well . . . I think I can remember the spell.

> Conceal, Conceal my Form so Fair
> Reveal me as a Chunk of Air . . .

Have I gone?

Father Christmas No. I'd better show you then. But not here.

Mabel No, we don't want anyone to see us being invisible.

Father Christmas We'll go somewhere private.

They move towards the door

Mabel (*as they move*) Have you ever disappeared in public?

Father Christmas Oh yes. At Christmas I usually make several public disappearances.

Mabel That's very clever.

Father Christmas One Christmas I was so clever I didn't appear at all.

They go into the Palace

Music, variation of tune

Abel and Violet dance on, planting clues all over the stage. Abel pops one into the hat of the Snowman. They exit

Criss-cross entrances for the Company, each carrying a clue and being led on to another with which they exit. Burgess, Alison and Mr Ough are prominent in this

Henrietta is seen to be hunting everywhere for hers. She is left alone, still unable to find it. The music fades

Edward enters

Edward Henrietta! There you are. I've been looking for you everywhere.

Henrietta Edward! Why are you still in evening dress? And why were you looking for me? You should be looking for your clues.

Edward I don't need to.

Father Christmas (*off, his voice booming over the mike*) No search . . . No suit . . . No happiness!

Edward (*under his breath*) Oh shut up! Have you found a clue yet, Henrietta?

Henrietta (*miserable*) No. And the others seem to be getting on so well.

Edward Couldn't we search *together*?
Father Christmas (*off*) It's against the Rules!
Henrietta There. I'm sorry, Edward.
Edward It's all right. Just thought it'd be more fun with two of us, that's all.
Henrietta Good luck, Edward.
Edward I hope you find what you're looking for, Henrietta.

He exits, rather sadly

Henrietta I know exactly what I'm looking for. (*She takes the bottle out of her bag and gazes at it*) Dr Beamish! But where to look, that's the difficulty.

The Snowman sneezes

What's that? (*She hastily puts the bottle back in her bag*) Someone sneezed.

The Snowman sneezes again, louder. Henrietta whirls round

It seemed to come from over there.

The Snowman moves slightly

Why Snowman, I do believe it was you! (*She runs upstage of him*) You sneezed for a purpose didn't you?

The Snowman shakes his head

You mean you've caught a cold?

The Snowman nods

Oh I am sorry. All the same—something tells me—of course! It's *you*! *You* can tell me. You know where my clue is, don't you?

The Snowman shifts a little

You do! I thought so. Oh please, dear Snowman, tell me. Talk to me. Speak to me.

Song 11: Speak to Me, Snowman

During the intro Henrietta wheels the Snowman round so that he faces the audience. He makes a stupendous effort to talk

Snowman	Ooba-ooba-ooba-ooba—
Henrietta	Speak to me, Snowman!
Snowman	Ooba-ooba-ooba-ooba—
Henrietta	Speak to me, Snowman!

The Cousins, intrigued to see the Snowman come to life, gather to watch

	Can't you ever utter things?
	Or can you only stutter things?
	(Like Burgess)
Snowman	Ooba-ooba-ooba-ooba—
Henrietta	All you have to do is—

Snowman	Ooba-ooba-ooba-ooba—
Henrietta	Tell me where my clue is
Cousins	Can't you ever blabber words
	That aren't just jibber-jabber words?
Henrietta	Poor thing!
Cousins	He's quivering, shivering
Henrietta	Poor thing!
Cousins	He's suffering from cold
Henrietta	To cure your influenza
	Sing us a Cadenza!
Cousins	He may be too frozen
	He may be too old.

The Snowman, stung by this remark, attempts a cadenza. It fails and he relapses into his "Ooba's" over which Henrietta sings:

Henrietta	He's too cold to talk, but there might be a chance
	If I could persuade him to dance!
Cousins	Dance! Dance!
Snowman	Ooba-ooba-ooba-ooba—
Henrietta	Dance with me Snowman!
Snowman	Ooba-ooba-ooba-ooba—
Henrietta	Dance with me Snowman!
Cousins	Let Henrietta warm you
	Then it might transform you
	Then you might be voluble
	The situation's soluble
Henrietta	If I could have the pleasure
	Of a dance——
	Mr Snowman!

The Snowman bows stiffly and he and Henrietta dance, slowly at first, then faster and faster with the Cousins clapping them on. Finally the dance becomes so heated that Henrietta falls back exhausted and the Snowman, after a gurgle or two, melts into the ground. (The Snowman's costume should be like a collapsible bell-tent. If he can melt down a trap in the stage—with only his head at stage level—so much the better. Otherwise he must sink as far as possible on to his knees)

(*Speaking*) Oh what have I done? I've melted him.

Rosie Henrietta, how dreadful!

Biddie Nothing left but a heap of snow.

Dora And a pipe and a hat.

Henrietta Oh dear! But wait a minute. There's something *in* the hat. It's a clue! With my name on it. So that's why! Go away everybody. I have to open this by myself. It's my first clue, and I'm sure it must be very special.

Edith (*as she goes with the others*) Lucky you! You must remember to melt people more often.

The Cousins exit

Henrietta opens the clue and reads:

Henrietta   "Be not nervous, be not squeamish
                       Ask the Doctor, known as Beamish."

Well! What good is that sort of clue? Of course I want to ask the Doctor! I
want to ask him to marry me, actually. (*She opens her bag and takes out the
bottle again*) Oh my dear Dr Beamish, I'm no nearer finding you than I
was before. (*Reading*) "Available at all chemists, three shillings and
twopence a bottle." But what's this? In tiny letters. "Also, direct from the
Inventor, seventy-seven Fir Tree Lane." Thank you, dear Snowman, you
have given me a clue after all. Now I know what I must find. Seventy-
seven Fir Tree Lane. (*She is about to go, then turns back*) Oh . . . but I can't
leave you in that condition. What you need is a good pick-me-up. But of
course! I have the very thing for you.

*She brandishes the bottle and gives the remains of the Snowman a taste of it.
To a weird version of the "Snowman" tune he begins to rise again and
eventually resumes his original shape. He bows to Henrietta*

   She kisses him and goes

The music of "Umbrella Song" is heard

   *Burgess enters reading a clue and swinging his umbrella. Alison enters
   pursuing him*

Alison Burgess! Burgess! what does your clue say?

Burgess hums

   Mine says "Find Henrietta".

Burgess whistles

            "Find Henrietta and be of good cheer,
            From her you'll discover the field is clear."

I've looked for her everywhere, but she seems to have disappeared.

Burgess stops whistling

Burgess What did you say?
Alison I said, she seems to have disappeared.
Burgess (*alarmed*) But that's impossible. (*A twirl of the umbrella restores his
confidence*) Oh well, she's certain to turn up soon. (*He hums again*)
Alison Are you—you are expecting her?

He hums louder

   Oh Burgess, I do wish you'd stop humming and tell me what your clue
   says.
Burgess We're not supposed to tell, you know, but since you've blurted out
yours—(*He opens his clue and reads*) "Do not scorn a Lass Love-lorn."
Alison (*delighted*) Why Burgess, you know what that means don't you?
Burgess Naturally. I've long suspected Henrietta was suffering on my
account.

Alison Henrietta. Oh I see. (*She droops*)

Burgess does a few tango steps with his umbrella

Burgess Most girls seem to fall for me sooner or later. (*He elaborates his dance a little, using the umbrella as a willing partner*) I suppose I have got a certain air.

With a final dashing gesture he hangs the umbrella on the arm of the Snowman who immediately moves off with it, swinging it jauntily

Alison Oh yes Burgess, you *have*.
Burgess (*looking round wildly*) Have what?
Alison A certain air. (*Moving close to him*) In fact I find you quite bewilderingly fascinating. (*She yearns at him*)
Burgess (*terrified*) Oh no, Alison. No, no, no. You're quite wrong. No woman ever falls for me. I suppose I'm just not attractive.
Alison Burgess whatever is the matter with you?
Burgess I could kill that Snowman I really could. (*Looking all over the place*) Oh where has he got to, the thieving brute?
Alison What are you talking about?
Burgess Nothing, nothing. I must find Henrietta before it's too late.
Alison Before *what's* too late?
Burgess I can feel everything slipping away from me.
Alison (*flinging her arms round him*) Not me Burgess! I'll never slip away from you!

Music. Burgess struggles to free himself. They wrestle

Song 12: Speak to Me (Reprise)

Burgess	I-I-I-I-I-I-I-I——
Alison	Speak to me Burgess!
Burgess	I-I-I-I-I-I-I-I——
Alison	Speak to me Burgess!
	Can't you ever utter things?
	Or can you only stutter things
	Like——
Burgess	I-I-I-I-I-I-I-I——
Alison	Talk to me kindly!
Burgess	I-I-I-I-I-I-I-I——
Alison	I adore you blindly!
	Let my ardour warm you
	Then it might transform you
	Then you might be voluble
	The situation's soluble
	If only you would speak one tender word
	Dearest Burgess!

Burgess breaks free on the last note and runs off

Alison wilts

From the other side, Henrietta and Mr Ough enter

Henrietta Haven't you any idea where seventy-seven Fir Tree Lane is, Father?

Mr Ough None at all.

Henrietta Oh dear! Oh hello Alison.

Alison (*tearfully*) Burgess has been looking for you.

Henrietta (*disinterested*) Has he?

Alison And so have I, as a matter of fact, because of my clue. Have you got a clue, Uncle Arthur?

Mr Ough Yes. Not a very helpful one though.
> "Be not vague nor unstable,
> Find Abel, ask Abel."

Henrietta I keep telling you, Father, where *your* happiness lies. A proposal. You've got to bring yourself to *propose*.

Mr Ough What? To Abel?

Henrietta No, *Mabel*. Don't you think so, Alison?

Alison Oh yes, Uncle Arthur. Aunt Mabel's very fond of you.

Mr Ough (*pleased*) Oh is she? Then why does this say Abel? They've left out the M perhaps.

Henrietta No, no. Nothing's allowed to be too easy.

Alison So first you find Abel——

Henrietta And then Mabel.

Mr Ough (*totally fogged*) Abel ... Mabel ...

Henrietta And when you do find her, Father, dance with her. It's easy to propose while you're dancing.

Mr Ough Is it? Oh very well, if you say so my dear ... Abel ... Mabel ...

He goes off muttering

The girls laugh, then sigh

Henrietta His problem's quite simple isn't it?

Alison Yes. Henrietta, I have to consult *you* about my clue.

Henrietta Oh?

Alison Yes, it says:
> "Find Henrietta and be of good cheer,
> From her you'll discover the field is clear."

Henrietta How very strange! What are you searching for Alison?

Alison (*taking a locket out of her bag*) The man I love.

Henrietta But how can I help?

Alison I don't know. It seems hopeless since you love him too.

Henrietta *I* love him? Who are we talking about?

Alison shows her the locket and Henrietta gives a startled little giggle

Why it's Burgess.

Alison Why did you give that startled little giggle?

Henrietta (*laughing outright*) The idea of your thinking I was in love with Burgess!

Alison (*stiffly*) Thank you Henrietta. You have been *most* helpful. (*She snatches back the locket*) I quite understand why I was told to consult you.

And now I don't think I need to trouble you any further. (*She begins to go*)

Henrietta Oh Alison wait! I'm so sorry. I know Burgess is *very* nice—and some people think he's quite good-looking—but you see I'm searching for someone else.

Alison (*mollified*) The man you love?

Henrietta Yes. Here he is.

She shows the bottle to Alison who gasps and bursts out laughing

Alison Why it's nothing but a bottle of tonic!

Henrietta (*severely*) Elixir.

Alison Oh but darling Henrietta, all that *hair*! You can't, you simply can't be in love with him. (*Taking out the locket again*) I mean you only have to put the two side by side to see how absurd it is.

Henrietta I agree.

Alison moves away from her, gazing at Burgess's picture, and speaks half to herself

Alison Poor Henrietta! Oh Burgess, Burgess, how could you waste your affections on a girl who has evidently lost all her judgment?

Henrietta (*similarly half-aside*) Poor Alison! She may think me some sort of Delilah, but personally I would prefer to be in love with a man whose strength lay in his hair rather than in his umbrella.

Song 13: Poor Henrietta, Poor Alison

Alison	Poor Henrietta!
Henrietta	Poor Alison!
Both	Oh what a sad, sad waste!
	She's a sweet delightful girl
	But without much taste.
Alison	Poor Henrietta!
Henrietta	Poor Alison!
Both	Why does she peak and pine
	For a man who can't compare
	With a man like mine!
Alison	I always believed her judgment good
	Now I must clearly think again
Henrietta	I always admired her taste in clothes
	But I deplore her taste in men.
Alison	Poor Henrietta!
Henrietta	Poor Alison!
Both	Loves with a love misplaced
	She's a dear romantic girl
	But without much taste
Alison	Poor Henrietta!
Henrietta	Poor Alison

Both   Ought to have drawn the line
                  At a man so far beneath
                  Any man like man
                  Every girl should be in love
                  With a man like mine.

They exchange a parting kiss, and Alison goes

The music modulates. Henrietta sighs

Henrietta Seventy-seven Fir Tree Lane. It sounds like somewhere in the City. And here I am in Christmasland. Oh why did I have to fall in love with someone so *difficult*?

Reprise: A Face In A Photograph

During this reprise a huge blow-up of the "Moonshine" advertisement appears on the stage behind Henrietta, either wheeled on by Abel and Disabel, or possibly propelled from the back by Father Christmas who is concealed behind it. The picture of "Dr Beamish" obviously dominates the advertisement but the lettering and decoration should make it look as much like a magazine advert of 1910 as possible

(*Singing*)   But when I first saw him
                   He looked at me
                   As no-one had looked at me before
                   He's only a face in a photograph
                   But he is the man I adore.

Abel brings on a signpost saying "77 Fir Tree Lane" which he sets down, pointing at the advertisement. He taps Henrietta on the shoulder and skips off

Henrietta sees first the sign and then the photograph

(*Speaking*) Oh . . . Oh . . . it's *him*! It's Dr Beamish! But where is he? And where am I! (*She goes closer to the advert and calls, rather nervously*) Hallo! Hallo! Is anybody there?

Father Christmas comes from behind the advert. He is disguised in white overalls as a very old chemist.

Father Christmas Yes, yes. What is it?
Henrietta (*disconcerted*) I've—I've come to enquire about . . . (*She takes the bottle out*) about "Moonshine".
Father Christmas Yes?
Henrietta This *is* seventy-seven Fir Tree Lane, isn't it?
Father Christmas Yes, yes.
Henrietta And you do make "Moonshine" here?
Father Christmas Of course we do. We do nothing else.
Henrietta Then I wonder if you can tell me—where is Dr Beamish?
Father Christmas Here. I am Dr Beamish.
Henrietta (*horrified*) But the photograph . . . and it says here on the bottle——

Father Christmas Oh *him*! He's a nobody. Just there for advertisement. A model we picked from an agency.

Henrietta (*stifling tears*) How disgraceful! How dishonest!

Father Christmas Just a minute, young lady, you could hardly expect *me* to sit for the photograph could you? (*Indicating the advert*) "Tired and Worried ... Nervous and Irritable ... Feeling your Age?" Well isn't that exactly what I look like? What I *am*, in fact. No, no, when it comes to advertising one must be realistic—I mean one must *never* be realistic.

Henrietta So the whole thing's a fake.

Father Christmas By no means. After all, this—(*Pointing to the photograph*)—is what interested you in the first place, isn't it?

Henrietta (*taking her handkerchief out*) Oh yes indeed. I was very, very interested.

Father Christmas And that's why you were carrying this bottle around with you, wasn't it?

Henrietta Yes.

Father Christmas Without even touching a drop?

Henrietta No, I've never tasted it.

Father Christmas There you are. Sold on the product without trying it. That's good advertising.

Henrietta But now that I know that *my* Dr Beamish isn't *you*, Dr Beamish, is in fact a model and not a Dr Beamish at all, what am I to do about it, Dr Beamish?

Father Christmas (*shrugging*) Find the model, I suppose.

Henrietta But how? Oh please help me. I'm so miserable.

Father Christmas (*clapping his hands*) Miss Brightface! Miss Jolly! Demonstration please. We have a customer.

Music. Mabel and Violet enter, dressed as two laboratory assistants, wheeling on a chemical contraption for making "Moonshine". (This should be a pantomime-prop arrangement of curling test-tubes, very bizarre and old-fashioned. If possible, we should be able to see blue liquid poured in one end and frothing out at the other!) The amount of business connected with the prop depends on the nature of it

Song 14: Try a Little Bit of Moonshine

Mabel	Are you tired? Are you worried?
Violet	Are you nervous? Are you flurried?
	Are you feeling in a mood?
	Are you pale and off your food?
	Is your situation chronic?
	Are you longing for a tonic?
	Something to make you strong,
	Something to help you along?
Father Christmas	Then listen——
Mabel	Listen——
Violet	Listen——
All 3	To our song!

Father Christmas	Try a little bit of moonshine!
	Who needs sunshine?
	Just a little bit of moonshine
	Does you so much good
	Doesn't matter if it's lunchtime
	Doesn't matter if it's teatime
	A jolly little bit of moonshine
	Gives you
	What no doctor could!

Mabel and Violet join him in repeating this verse to Henrietta's growing frustration and despair

All 3	Try a little bit of moonshine . . . *etc.*

They try to tempt Henrietta to taste it but she refuses

Father Christmas	Doesn't have to be at night-time
Mabel	The day-time——
Violet	Is play-time
All 3	When moonshine shines on you.
Father Christmas	Doesn't matter if it's bed-time
Mabel	Or bath-time——
Violet	Or laugh-time——
All 3	All you have to do—is——
	Try a little bit of moonshine!
	Who needs sunshine?
	Just a little bit of moonshine's
	Better than a rest
	Doesn't matter if it's Monday
	Saturday or even Sunday
	A jolly little bit of moonshine—
	Moonshine! Moonshine!
	Makes you feel you're at your sunny best.

Henrietta, exasperated by their cheerfulness, and totally disillusioned, throws down the bottle and runs off

Father Christmas and Mabel congratulate each other, then they and Violet wheel off the advertisement and the "Moonshine" prop while they sing

Father Christmas	*(together)*	Doesn't have to be at Christmas
Mabel		Can be any that or this-mas
Violet		A jolly little bit of moonshine—
		Moonshine! Moonshine!
		Makes—you—feel—you're—
		At—your—sunny—best!

They exit

Music changes to a minor key

Eustace, Sidney, Rosie, Biddie, Dora and Edith enter carrying Uncle Charles who is frozen stiff in a sitting position. They put him down and he slowly rolls over

Song 15: Try a Little Bit of Moonshine (Reprise)

Cousins	Poor Uncle Charles is frozen stiff
(*lines divided*)	Because he wouldn't look for clues
	He and Father Christmas must have had a tiff
	What is the remedy to use?
	Have we any brandy handy? No.
	Have we any whisky to make him frisky?
	What's that bottle lying there?
	Where? There! Take care!
	Let's try that on him! Do we dare?
	Of course we do! Of course we do!
	It's moonshine! Moonshine?
	A bottle of elixir
	That promises to fix 'yer
	This may see him through the worst
	He'll either survive alive
	Or burst!

During the first part of the refrain they put the bottle to Charles's lips as if feeding a baby. Very gradually Charles begins to unfreeze

> Try a little bit of moonshine!
> Who needs sunshine?
> Just a little bit of moonshine
> Does you so much good
> Doesn't matter if it's lunch-time
> Doesn't matter if it's tea-time
> A jolly little bit of moonshine
> Gives you
> What no doctor could!

Charles, creaking with the effort of returning to life, sings haltingly:

Charles	Doesn't have to be at night-time——
	The day-time—is play-time——
Cousins	Now moonshine shines in you
Charles	Doesn't matter if it's bed-time——
Cousins	Or bath-time——
Charles	Or laugh-time (*he chuckles unexpectedly*)
Cousins	All you have to do—is——

Charles grabs the bottle and takes a huge swig. He is transformed into a picture of jollity

Charles	Try a little bit of moonshine!
	Who needs sunshine?

All   Just a little bit of moonshine's
                     Better than a rest
                     Doesn't have to be at Christmas——
Charles   Can be any that or this-mas——
All   A jolly little bit of moonshine
                     Moonshine! Moonshine!
                     Makes—you—feel—you're——
                     At—your—sunny—best!

They exit, dancing gleefully, Charles last, doing a scissor jump as he goes

Father Christmas and Mabel enter, themselves again

Father Christmas Things are going rather well, don't you think? Rather well. Did you see Charles? I told you I'd get him smiling.

Mabel And what about poor Henrietta? All her illusions shattered in the snow.

Father Christmas Don't *worry* so much, Mabel, about other people. Leave that to me; remember you have your own happiness to think of.

Mr Ough enters studying his clue

The others withdraw

Mr Ough   "Be not vague, or unstable,
                    Find Abel, ask Abel"

Yes, that's all very well, but where is the lad?

Abel appears (beckoned by Father Christmas) with a clue on a salver

Mr Ough takes it

(*Reading*) "Abel present—well done Abel!
             Now do your bit—Dance with Mabel."

Abel exits

Of course! That's exactly what Henrietta told me to do. I must find Mabel. (*He wanders round looking*)

Father Christmas (*whispering, aside*) Now Mabel. Now's your chance.

Mabel You mean—he might propose?

Father Christmas As long as you make it difficult enough for him.

Mabel But I'd like to make it easy.

Father Christmas No, no. Men like him have to be goaded. Go on, now. And good luck.

He pushes Mabel forward and exits

Mabel takes up her best ballet position

Mabel Good-evening, Arthur.

Mr Ough (*passing her*) Good-evening. (*He raises his hat, hurries on, then double-takes*) Good heavens! It's you!

Mabel Yes, Arthur.

Mr Ough But Mabel—you're a *fairy*!

Mabel (*limbering*) Does it make any difference?

Mr Ough N-no. Only——

Mabel Only what?

Mr Ough I think I'm supposed to dance with you.

Mabel Well?

Mr Ough I'm not much of a dancer at the best of times—and this sort of stuff——

Mabel Oh please Arthur, do partner me. I can't seem to get my fouettes right.

Mr Ough Your—?

Mabel These. (*She shows him*)

Mr Ough When you said "partner" Mabel, it reminded me of something I wanted to ask you——

Mabel (*doing a slow arabesque*) Yes?

Mr Ough You're making it very difficult for me to concentrate.

Mabel Help me with my arabesque, Arthur.

Mr Ough Arab what?

Mabel (*wobbling*) Quick Arthur. Take my hand ... that's it ... now, if you hold my waist ...

Mr Ough Like this?

Mabel I can keep on my point.

Mr Ough So you can!

Mabel There! I'll just show you, then we can dance together beautifully. Hold my waist.

Mr Ough So that you can keep to the point—er, on your point.

Mabel Now we can do a revolving arabesque.

Mr Ough Oh can we?

Mabel Just revolve, Arthur.

He does so, on his own

No, no. Don't let go.

He takes her waist again

Now ... that's right. Now I take up an attitude.

Mr Ough I'm not sure I like your attitude.

Mabel Take my hands ... the other way round ... Good! Dégagé.

Mr Ough I beg your pardon?

Mabel Open up.

Mr Ough Open—? Oh yes.

Mabel Pas de cheval.

Mr Ough Ah, I know what that means. It means "no horses".

Mabel No, Arthur. "Step of a horse"—like this. (*She shows him*)

Mr Ough I see. Like a hoof. (*He paws the ground*)

Mabel That's right. Now, lift from the waist, like this. (*Several tries— heaving noises*) Try again—One! Two! Threeee!

He lifts her beautifully and supports her

Mr Ough How long do I—?
Mabel Let me down gently.
Mr Ough Gently. Yes.

He lets her down with care and she sinks slowly on to her knees

That's not quite right, is it? I'm so sorry.
Mabel (*brightly*) No that was my fault. I forgot to unbend my knees. Now!
A chassé passé, a fall, a pirouette, and we're home!
Mr Ough I wish we were. Did you say a fall?
Mabel Not yet. (*In action*) Chassé passé to the right, to the left—now *fall*!

Mr Ough falls

No, Arthur, I fall and you catch me.
Mr Ough Oh.

They do it quite well

Mabel There! It's quite easy, isn't it? To the right . . . to the left . . .
Mr Ough Yes, it *is* easy . . .

He goes to the right when she falls to the left. She crashes

Oh Mabel, I am sorry.
Mabel (*getting up and dusting herself*) Never mind. These little accidents
happen at first.
Mr Ough (*depressed*) At first.
Mabel Now a pirouette. Turn me.
Mr Ough Turn you?
Mabel As if I was on a spit. (*She pirouettes*) So! And we finish.

There is a drum roll

Raise your right arm for a final flourish . . . no, no, gracefully, Arthur.
There! We go together beautifully.
Mr Ough Oh *yes* Mabel. And that's what I wanted to talk to you about . . .
Mabel Shall we take it straight through, then?
Mr Ough (*sighing*) Very well.

The dance is brief now and fairly smooth

Mabel Right! We begin with a fouetté, don't we?
Mr Ough Yes.

The dance begins

There's something I want to say, Mabel—I've always wanted to——
Mabel Revolve.
Mr Ough I feel the time has come for me to——
Mabel Revolve.
Mr Ough I've always admired you——
Mabel Attitude.
Mr Ough Put it this way——

They leap from right to left

Mabel This way.

Mr Ough This way——
Mabel This way.
Mr Ough Put it this way. I'm quite a weak person, Mabel——
Mabel Lift.
Mr Ough But I feel——
Mabel (*busily*) Chassé-passé to the left, to the right, to the left, to the right—(*Poised for a fall*) You were saying Arthur?
Mr Ough I——

She falls suddenly. He catches her in time

You make me feel—(*Catching her* L) You make me feel——

He catches her R. *He holds her, swaying against him in the "swan" attitude*

You make me feel——

Panting, as they sway mournfully

—so jolly.
Mabel (*dreamily*) I'm glad.
Mr Ough Mabel, will you——

She suddenly pirouettes—as she turns each time

Will you—will you—will you—?
Mabel (*briefly poised, face close to him*) Will I what?
Mr Ough It doesn't matter.

He stomps off disconsolately

Father Christmas enters

Father Christmas Congratulations.
Mabel What on?
Father Christmas Your dancing of course. (*He brings out a small bouquet*) Some Christmas roses for you.
Mabel (*taking them rather sullenly*) Thank you.
Father Christmas He didn't propose?
Mabel How could he? I didn't give him a chance, poor man.
Father Christmas (*rubbing his hands*) Good! Then next time he'll really mean it.
Mabel How do I know there'll be a next time? Really Father Christmas, I'm beginning to think you don't *want* any of us to be happy.
Father Christmas (*wagging his finger*) A-ah! Impatience! None of that. Everything's going according to plan. Ssh! Out of the way. Here comes Henrietta.
Mabel Crying, by the looks of it. Are you sure you know what you're doing?

They exit

Henrietta enters attempting to read a clue through her tears

Henrietta I'm beginning to think Father Christmas doesn't want any of us to be happy. I've been trying to follow the clues but they don't seem to lead anywhere. (*Reading*)

"Count from the Palace the third little tree
Wait there and Two will be company."

She starts to do this

Edward enters, in his new suit now, with clue

Edward (*reading*)   "Count from the Palace the third little tree
Wait there and Two will be company."

They meet back to back

Henrietta!

Henrietta Edward!

Edward Mine says wait here and two will be company.

Henrietta So does mine.

Edward Then it must mean you.

Henrietta How odd! Do you think it's a mistake?

Edward No. I told you we should be searching together. Perhaps we're both after the same thing.

Henrietta I'm looking for the person I love.

Edward So am I.

Henrietta Oh Edward! And does this clue help you?

Edward Yes.

Henrietta It doesn't help me at all.

Edward It doesn't? Oh. Goodbye, Henrietta. (*He begins to go*)

Henrietta Edward! Where are you going?

Edward Back to Earth, if I can. Tobago, Sierra Leone, Brixton—anywhere.

Henrietta Don't go. I've—I've got used to you being around.

Edward What's the point? I'm afraid my search is hopeless.

Henrietta Why?

Edward Because you are the person I love, Henrietta.

Henrietta (*with intense dismay*) Oh dear!

Edward Never mind. It's all in the game. You love someone else and you're looking for him and there we are.

Henrietta Yes. (*Seeking to comfort him*) It's someone I've never met, Edward.

Edward Oh? But you've seen him, surely?

Henrietta Yes. But I threw him away.

Edward (*puzzled*) Threw him away?

Henrietta He was on the bottle, you see ...

Edward What?!!

Henrietta Stuck to it. A photograph—an advertisement—do you think I'm silly?

Edward N-no. I suppose he's sort of romantic-looking?

Henrietta He is a bit.

Edward (*turning away*) I thought so.

Henrietta Oh Edward ...

Song 16: I'd Love To Be In Love With You

(*Singing*) I'm sorry I don't love you
I apologize
You're sweet and understanding
And charming and wise
If I had not already chosen
You'd be the one I would choose
I'm honoured to know
You love me so
It's breaking my heart to refuse.

I'd love to be in love with you
In love with you, in love with you,
I'd love to be in love with you
But my heart is not my own
If I could be in love with you
In love with you, in love with you
If I could be in love with you
We need not search alone.

Both We wouldn't be
So lost and lonely
Our lives would be complete
If only—

$\left. \begin{array}{l} \text{I} \\ \text{You} \end{array} \right\}$ had the heart to be in love with $\left\{ \begin{array}{l} \text{you} \\ \text{me} \end{array} \right.$

In love with $\left\{ \begin{array}{l} \text{you} \\ \text{me} \end{array} \right\}$ in love with $\left\{ \begin{array}{l} \text{you} \\ \text{me} \end{array} \right.$

The heart to be in love with $\left\{ \begin{array}{l} \text{you} \\ \text{me} \end{array} \right.$

But $\left\{ \begin{array}{l} \text{my} \\ \text{your} \end{array} \right\}$ heart is not $\left\{ \begin{array}{l} \text{my} \\ \text{your} \end{array} \right\}$ own

Burgess enters, running

Burgess D-d-d-dear Henrietta! At last I've found you!

Henrietta Burgess, you're so out of breath.

Burgess I've been running and running and missing you everywhere. L-l-listen. I've had a clue. It says "Do not scorn a Lass Love-lorn". That's you Henrietta.

Henrietta Me?

Burgess You're love-lorn aren't you? P-p-please tell me you're love-lorn!

Henrietta Well, I——

Edward She is, old fruit, but not for you.

Burgess What?

Edward Not for you—or me either.

Burgess What have you got to do with it?

Edward The same as you.

Burgess What do you m-m-m-ean?
Edward We're in the same b-b-b-boat.
Henrietta Ssh! Dear Burgess, there *is* a lass who loves you.
Burgess Not you?
Henrietta No, someone else. Why don't you look for her?
Burgess But Henrietta—who are you talking about?

Alison enters, with Burgess's umbrella, wailing

Alison Burgess! Burgess!
Burgess Oh, her!
Alison Don't turn away from me Burgess. I've found your umbrella.
Burgess You have? (*He takes it, twirls it for a moment, then pushing Alison aside, advances wolfishly on Henrietta*) Now look here, Henrietta—don't be a little fool—you know very well you find me attractive—
Alison Oh!! (*She snatches the umbrella and breaks it*) *Bother* your beastly umbrella! (*She weeps*) I want to go home!
Burgess (*trying to piece the umbrella together and weeping too*) S-s-so do I!

Mr Ough enters, meeting Alison

Mr Ough I say, Alison, I've had the most extraordinary clue. It says "Do not scorn a Lass Love-lorn". Well now, I don't know very many lasses——

Mabel appears at his side and taps him on the shoulder

Oh hello Mabel. Recovered from our exertions? (*To Alison*) As I was saying, I don't seem to know very many lasses and I wondered if it might be you by any chance?

Alison whimpers

Of course I know you're a relative, but *many* times removed ...

Alison howls

Mabel Oh *really*!
Mr Ough (*looking from one to the other in confused dismay*) I wish I was at home with a good book.

Wild singing of the "Moonshine" song is heard. Uncle Charles enters, supported by the Cousins

Eustace I think we'd better take Uncle Charles home.
Edith He's been behaving very strangely.
Mabel What's the matter with him?
Charles I'm happy Mabel, happy. That's what's the matter with me.
Burgess Disg-g-gusting!
Sidney A little bit too much Moonshine I'm afraid.
Edward Moonshine? Did you say Moonshine?
Henrietta So he had it!
Rosie (*holding up the bottle*) Look, the bottle's quite empty.
Henrietta (*taking it*) And the photograph's all messed up and spoiled. I can hardly see it any more.

Edward (*moving to her*) Henrietta——

Henrietta No Edward, don't speak to me. Don't anyone speak to me. I just want to go home. (*She runs to Mabel*)

Mabel (*holding her*) Darling!

Henrietta Oh Aunt Mabel, you can do magic just as well as him. Can't you get us home?

Alison Yes, do, Aunt Mabel, do!

Burgess P-p-p-lease!

General pleading cries

Mabel Well, darlings, I'll *try*. It may be difficult—even dangerous—but I'll *try*!

The Company group round her expectantly

If only I can remember the Magic Gesture—the one that he makes ...

Mood music. She tries a Gesture. Nothing happens. The Company sigh and change position. She tries a second Gesture. Still nothing happens. An audible groan and change of position. Nerving herself for a special effort she makes a third Gesture. Dramatic lighting change and the Company freeze like statues, each turned towards the one he or she is searching for

Oh what have I done? I've done something dreadful! I believe I've frozen them all.

In alarm she tries several frantic Gestures that have no effect whatever

Oh my dears, I *am* so sorry! (*To the audience*) I'm not sure they can even hear me. I should never have tried this on my own. (*She darts hither and thither*) Father Christmas! Help! Where are you? Father Christmas! He doesn't answer. I expect he's angry with me. No wonder!

Faraway music. Gently it begins to snow

And now it's beginning to snow. If I don't get it right soon they'll all turn into snowmen. (*A thought strikes*) Snow! That reminds me of something ... some spell from my youth ... connected with snow ... I'm sure I learnt it for my Fairy Levels ... it's no good, it's gone from me. But the Book of Spells must still be in the Christmas Library. That's it! I must find it! I must find it at once!

She runs into the Palace

The music swells and the snow falls harder. Slowly the Company begin to sway to the rhythm. During the whole of the first part of the song they move as if in their own private world, unable to make contact with each other. Henrietta is the first to stir from the spot. One by one the others join her, but there is no connection between them as they come to shadowy life

Song 17: The Snowfall Waltz

Henrietta   It's hard to know the way to go
Burgess   We journey through the falling snow

Edward	We wander, searching to and fro
All 3	In the snowfall waltz
Charles ⎱	And as we circle everywhere
Mr Ough ⎰	
Alison	We seek the prize that's never there
All 5	Uncertainty is in the air
	In the snowfall waltz.
Alison	It's a game when you begin it
	Search for clues and then search for more
Henrietta	You believe that any minute
	You will find what you're searching for.

The whole Company now moves in a dream-like solitary waltz

All	But when the snow begins to fall
	The drifting swirl divides us all
	And no-one answers when we call
	In the snowfall waltz.

They freeze again into their first positions

Mabel hurries back on carrying the Book of Spells, with Abel and Disabel in attendance

Mabel My dears! I've found it! Here it is. Under "Christmas Day-Returns". I'm sure this is the spell we want. Listen. (*She reads*)

> "For Earthly Souls unwilling trapped
> This spell can prove extremely apt.
> When in this Land it starts to snow
> 'Tis not yet snowing down below.
> But when on Earth that snow doth fall
> It can mean Home for one and all."

Abel turns the page for her

> "All people that on Earth do dwell . . ."

No, no. That can't be right. Oh yes, it is.

> "All people that on Earth do dwell
> Should heed this interesting Spell
> For if they trust its Magic Worth
> 'Twill take them safely back to Earth."

So! Now—the Spell!

She hands the book to Disabel who almost collapses under the weight. Mabel gets herself into her best fairy position and chants, to the music:

> "Follow the Snow, Follow the Snow
> Down to Earth, and Home you go!"

"The Snowfall Waltz" plays again. Another sudden lighting change. The atmosphere is now bright and sparkling and the Company, no longer in a

dream, gather round Mabel, giddily welcoming the swirling snow as a symbol of their safe return home. Excited voices over magic, lines divided as appropriate

All Something's happening! She's done it! I feel as though I were falling. Yes, like a shower of snow. Like before. Only the other way round. I wonder if Father Christmas knows? He'll be livid you managed it without him. Serves him right for bringing us here in the first place. Oh Aunt Mabel, how clever you are!

(*Singing*)   Good for you! You've turned the tables!
                    On your own you have found the spell
                    Glory be for all Aunt Mabels!
                    Trust in them and then all is well.

During the final refrain Violet enters with a travelling cloak and a huge "Merry Widow" hat which she helps Mabel into to form the picture for the Curtain

                    You've shown us how, and now we know
                    The way to home, and home we go!
                    We're falling homeward with the snow
                    In the snowfall, snowfall,
                    Snowfall, snowfall waltz!

CURTAIN

ACT III

Mabel's drawing-room

When the CURTAIN *rises, the whole Company is on, except Edward, Charles and Father Christmas. They are in exactly the same positions as they were at the end of Act I when the magic began to happen. The cracker is open and the clues are strewn over the floor. For a moment there is a frozen tableau, then a buzz of activity and rapid conversation*

Henrietta A treasure-hunt! How exciting!

Mr Ough Good idea of yours, Mabel.

Mabel Yes, it was rather, wasn't it?

Alison I thought we were going to play "Sardines"—didn't you Burgess?

Burgess Or "Murder".

Henrietta This is much more fun. Do we open our clues now?

Mabel Yes, come along. Find your names.

Henrietta (*with a handful*) Rosie—Biddie . . .

Mr Ough I haven't got my spectacles. What does this say, dear?

Henrietta It says you, Father. (*She whispers*) "Ask Violet where the cat sleeps."

Mr Ough Ah!

Violet (*loudly*) Mine says "Look in the bathroom cupboard".

Mabel Hush, Violet. You're not supposed to say.

Violet (*clapping her hand to her mouth*) Sorry, madam.

Alison Aunt Mabel, here's a clue marked "Father Christmas". But we haven't got a Father Christmas this year, have we?

Henrietta Oh yes we have. A charming one.

Mr Ough Certainly we have. Cross and cold, but all togged up and ready for the fray.

Mabel Will somebody fetch him?

Henrietta ⎫ (*together*) ⎧ Of course. I'll go.
Mr Ough ⎭   ⎩

They go, one up L *one up* R

Laughter

Mabel Dear Arthur! Going the wrong way, as usual.

Henrietta enters with Edward, in his Father Christmas costume, and Mr Ough enters with Charles, in his

Henrietta ⎫ (*together*) ⎧ Here he is!
Mr Ough ⎭   ⎩

General consternation. During the following Edward and Charles approach each other, staring as if at a memory

Mabel Charles, you've come. How nice. How dare you? You're supposed to be in bed.

Henrietta Of course we're very glad you're better, Uncle Charles——

Mabel Are we?

Henrietta But you see Edward is being paid.

Mabel I'm so sorry, Mr Keene. This is most embarrassing.

Henrietta I really don't think there ought to be two of you.

Music of "There's Only One Father Christmas". Edward and Charles, as in a trance, repeat their dance routine. At the point where Father Christmas appeared before, they stop, stare at each other and then at the chimney. The music becomes "magical"

Mabel Charles! (*She passes a hand in front of his eyes*) Edward! What's the matter with you?

Edward I think I had a dream.

Charles So did I.

Edward Or rather I feel as if all this had happened before.

Henrietta So do I, Edward.

Alison So do I. Burgess——

Burgess I know, Alison. It's a strange feeling, isn't it?

Mabel What's come over you all? I think you need a drink. Abel! Disabel!

Abel and Disabel appear with trays of drinks

(*Gaily*) Burgess, a drink! Alison! Arthur, you look fish-like. What's the matter?

Mr Ough (*hypnotized*) Chassé-passé. (*He takes a drink*)

Mabel What?

Charles grabs a drink from Disabel

Charles (*loudly*) Moonshine!

All turn and look at him. Edward and Henrietta are visibly startled

Mabel (*to a Cousin*) There! He's taken a drink, and he *never* does usually. The party must be a success.

Edward Excuse me sir, what did you say just then?

Henrietta Yes, Uncle Charles, what did you say?

Charles (*beaming*) Moonshine.

Henrietta (*turning on Mabel, accusing*) Aunt Mabel, you *told* him! How could you? (*She turns away, clutching her bag to her breast*)

Charles, reliving a happy dream, begins to sway and sing:

Song 17A: Try a Little Bit of Moonshine (Reprise)

Charles   Try a little bit of moonshine!
                 Who needs sunshine?

> Just a little bit of moonshine's
> Better than a rest—

The Cousins join in, as memory returns to them. It also returns to Henrietta who stands downstage, miserable

Charles Cousins
> Doesn't have to be at Christmas
> Can be any that or this-mas
> A jolly little bit of moonshine
> Moonshine! Moonshine!
> Makes you feel you're at your sunny best!

Alison Uncle Charles! I've never seen you like this before.

Burgess Perhaps you haven't quite recovered from your influ-flu-flu——

Charles That's it! We flew! We all flew! And I was happy. I still am. Can't you understand that? I found it!

Henrietta The bottle? Yes, I know.

Alison And took to it by the looks of things.

Charles I found my happiness! Didn't you Henrietta?

Henrietta No.

Burgess (*gazing at Henrietta*) Nor I.

Alison (*gazing at Burgess*) Nor I.

Charles Arthur?

Mr Ough I don't *think* I did. But then I'm not sure I ever lost it.

The telephone rings in the chimney. Mabel answers it

Mabel Hello. Oh yes. We were expecting him. (*She puts the receiver back*) That was Rodney. He says the Master's on his way.

Mr Ough Mabel, I'm dreadfully confused. Who is Rodney, and who is the Master, and why have you got a telephone in your chimney?

Mabel Pas de cheval, Arthur.

Mr Ough automatically paws the ground

Henrietta Aunt Mabel, you knew didn't you? You've known all along about what happened. And it wasn't him that brought us to earth again, it was you. Confess.

Mabel Yes. But I'm so nervous about what he's going to say that I've been trying to pretend nothing happened.

Music 17b. Lighting change

Father Christmas comes down the chimney

All part to make way for him. He advances on Mabel dangerously

Father Christmas So! You're here.

Mabel (*laughing nervously*) Oh yes, I'm here. (*Aside*) I wish I wasn't.
> "Conceal, conceal my form so fair,
> Reveal me as a chunk of Air ..."

Father Christmas You're all here. Well, well, well.

Henrietta Father Christmas, it was my fault. I wanted to come home, you see——

Alison So did I.

Burgess So did I.

Mabel So—I tried a little magic.

Father Christmas You tried a little magic.

Mabel And it happened to work.

Father Christmas It happened to work.

Mabel (*quailing*) Yes . . . silly of me, you might say . . . vain, presumptuous, downright naughty——

Father Christmas (*with a mighty beam*) Congratulations! You did splendidly!

He heartily shakes her hand

Mabel Thank you. What a relief!

Father Christmas (*ebullient*) This is exactly what I intended. I wanted you to stand on your own two feet.

Mabel Oh yes, well I did. On my own two points, in fact. (*She smiles at Mr Ough*)

Henrietta But Father Christmas, *is* this what you intended? Christmasland was lovely, of course, but I don't think any of us found what we were looking for.

Father Christmas You will, my dear, you will. When I descend on a Christmas party you can be sure that it will all end happily.

Henrietta At the moment I don't quite see how.

Burgess Nor do I. And forgive me, sir, if I seem imper-per-pertinent, but why are *we* the favoured ones? Is it always an English party that you descend on?

Alison Oh no Burgess. I'm sure he includes the Empire.

Father Christmas I include everybody. At one and the same time.

Song 18: The Merry Gentleman

The Company, sensing that Father Christmas wishes to take the stage, settle themselves on any piece of furniture that happens to be there, or on the floor

(*Singing*)	Be it Greece or Scandinavia
	Be it Hong Kong or Belgravia
	You will find that my behaviour
	Never varies!
All	Never varies!
Father Christmas	I am here and there and everywhere
	Be it Timbuctoo or Delaware
	Be it Swaziland or Finisterre
	Or the Canaries.
All	The Canaries.
Father Christmas	Change the country! Change the language!
	Even change my name!
	Call me Santa—call me Nicholas—
	Don't if you can help it, it sounds ridicholas—
	Call me Christmas!
All	Christmas!

Father Christmas	Louder!
All	Christmas!
Father Christmas	Louder!
All (*yelling*)	Christmas!
Father Christmas	Better!

Christmastime's a merry time
And I the great big world will span
To make the world a merry world
For I'm a merry gentleman.

All
Christmastime's a merry time
And he the great big world will span
To make the world a merry world
For he's a merry gentleman.

Father Christmas
Heigh-ho, the holly berry!
May your Christmases be merry
May your peace and comfort grow
Underneath the mistletoe.

Christmastime's a merry time
And I do all that Christmas can
To make the world a merry world
For I'm a merry—

All
very very merry
Merry merry merry merry gentleman!

During the following sequence, suitable props are handed to Father Christmas from the tree: i.e. maracas for Latin America, coolie hat for China etc. Possibly Mabel might don a different paper hat for each country

Father Christmas
When Santa Claus goes to Santa Fe
He goes in a Latin-American way
He undulates his magic whip, so
The reindeer whinny a gay calypso.

All
O Santa! O Santa!
The reindeer do a syncopated canter
They always nearly upset the sleigh
When Santa Claus goes to Santa Fe!

Father Christmas
And when the children wake up
On Christmas *mañana*
Their stockings are topped
With a marzipan banana

All
And instead of "Gee up"
He cries "Olé!"
When Santa Claus
Goes to Santa Fe.

Father Christmas
Ay! Ay! Ay!

When to China Santa goee
Eeny meeny miny moee
He make Santa velly smallee

                    Santa hardly there at allee
                    Santa must be niminee-piminee
                    To get down a Chinese chiminee.

                    When I go to Switzerland
                    With a yodely—odely—O!
                    I bear in mind that it's a land
All   Of yodely—odely—O!
Father Christmas   I take each house a Christmas box—
All   With a yodel-odel-odel-odel-odel-odel-o!
Father Christmas   Containing six new cuckoo clocks
                    That go—"Cuckoo"
All   Cuckoo! Cuckoo!
Father Christmas   And so you see, at Christmastime,
                    I do whatever Christmas can
                    To make the world a merry world
                    For I'm a merry gentleman.

The Company form a standing group round him and address the audience

All   Heigh-ho, the holly berry!
                    May your Christmases be merry
                    May your peace and comfort grow
                    Underneath the mistletoe!

                    Christmastime's a merry time
                    And he does all that a Christmas can
                    To make the world a merry world
                    For he's a merry—
Father Christmas   Very, very merry—
All   Merry merry merry merry
                    Gentleman!

At the end of the song Father Christmas waves everyone off and finally goes himself, leaving Mr Ough and Mabel alone together

Mabel busies herself, clearing glasses and humming

Mr Ough Mabel ...

Mabel Yes?

Mr Ough You remember when we were dancing together ...

Mabel Yes, Arthur, I remember.

Mr Ough Well do you remember that at the time I was trying to remember something I wanted to ask you ...?

Mabel Were you, Arthur dear?

Mr Ough And you were making it very difficult for me to remember ...

Mabel *Was* I? I don't remember that.

Mr Ough But somehow that made me feel I had to remember. And now I have.

Mabel What?

Mr Ough Remembered.

Mabel (*stacking glasses*) Oh good. What was it you wanted to ask me, Arthur?

Mr Ough It's this. Mabel, will you—will you sit down and *listen*!

Mabel Oh my dear Arthur, I'm so sorry. (*She sits*) Yes?

Mr Ough Mabel, will you——

She jumps up and tidies another glass

   Mabel!

Mabel Yes?

Mr Ough You're not listening.

Mabel I am, dear. Will I what?

Mr Ough Will you marry me, Mabel?

Mabel Yes, of course. (*She polishes a glass*)

Mr Ough Er—what did you say?

Mabel I said "Yes, of course".

Mr Ough Oh.

Mabel Aren't you pleased?

Mr Ough Yes, of course. Only—you don't seem at all—taken aback or anything.

Mabel (*sitting*) No Arthur, I've been expecting it for years.

Mr Ough Then why——?

Mabel I had to make it difficult for you or you'd never have quite got round to asking me. (*She pats his hand*)

Mr Ough So you are fond of me?

Mabel Oh very. You make me feel——

Mr Ough Jolly?

Mabel Extremely jolly.

Mr Ough Is it a momentous occasion?

Mabel Very momentous. Thank you for asking me, Arthur. (*A cloud passes over her face*) There is just one little difficulty . . .

Mr Ough What is it? You're not changing your mind?

Mabel No, no.

Mr Ough You look worried.

Mabel I am a bit.

Song 19: Ough

(*Singing*)	I'm fond of you, dear Arthur, but ere I become involved There is one tiny problem which has never yet been solved The letters of your surname, dear, or so you have announced, Are O and U and G and H—well, how are they pronounced?
Mr Ough	I must confess, dear Mabel, I have not the least idea My parents never told me—they were vague as me, I fear.
Both	So if we were indivisible, as far as we can tell, We'd run the risk of being unpronounceable as well.
	Is it Ow, as in bough? Is it Oo, as in through?

> When you're out in good society
> To brandish a variety
> Of surnames is a vulgar thing to do.
> Is it off, as in cough?
> Is it uff, as in rough?
> When a name is four-dimensional
> It's far too unconventional
> A simple word like "Smith" would be enough.
>
> There seems to be a choice of four
> But don't let's get depressed
> We'll say them over to ourselves
> And pick the one that's best.

Mr Ough   Off?

Mabel   Uff?

Mr Ough   Oo?

Mabel   Ow?

Mr Ough }
Mabel }   Oh if only { I / you } had listened

To { my / your } name when { I was / you were } christened
We'd avoid the indecision of it now.

Mabel   I'm not too keen on fancy names; I'd hate to share my home
With "Marchbanks" spelt as "Marjoribanks", "Cholo-mondeley" or "Siddy-Bottome"
I don't expect too much, my dear, but this I do expect
A name you can pronounce with pride, and know that it's correct.

Mr Ough   My dearest girl, I sympathize. You naturally are wary
Of names one only ought to meet in a rhyming dictionary.

Mr Ough }
Mabel }   The situation, then, is this. { You're / I'm } not too keen to wed
A name which sounds a wee bit rude, whichever way it's said.

> Off? Uff? Oo? Ow? . . . *etc.*

Mr Ough   My ancestors—

Mabel   Well what of them?

Mr Ough   Were French, my dear, and so
Let's add a D apostrophe

Both   And call our surname "D'Ough"!

Mr Ough   D'Ough?

Mabel   D'Ough?

Mr Ough   D'Ough?

Mabel   D'Ough?

Both   Though it sounds a trifle bready
I am fond of it already
It's the nicest monosyllable I know

Thank you, thank you D apostrophe!
You've saved us from catostrophe
By turning us so neatly into dough.

They retire

Song 20: The Umbrella Song (Reprise—dance)

As they do so, Burgess and Alison enter dancing. Burgess is having difficulty. He trips more and more seriously and finally gives up

Burgess It's no g-g-g-good, Alison. We'd better stop.
Alison Oh *no*, Burgess.
Burgess I'm so bad at it. It's no fun for you.
Alison It *is*! I *love* it when you tread on my toes.
Burgess You're k-k-k-kidding me.
Alison I wouldn't kid you, Burgess. I love you too much.
Burgess Everyone's always kidding me——
Alison Burgess, did you hear what I said?
Burgess I'm just a laughing-stock——
Alison I said I *love* you, Burgess——
Burgess (*still not hearing*) I don't know why I don't d-d-drown myself.
    Nobody wants me——
Alison (*shouting*) I'm a *lass love-lorn*!
Burgess Sssh! Don't shout Alison.
Alison Why shouldn't I shout?
Burgess It sounds so loud.
Alison Dear Burgess, I've brought you a Christmas Present. (*She gets it from behind the tree*) Will you have it now?
Burgess (*dismally*) Thank you very much.
Alison Well, open it. (*He opens the parcel and takes out a very small umbrella*)
Burgess I say, it's a sort of umbrella. I say! Thank you. (*Doubtfully*) It's wonderful. (*With difficulty he makes the gestures he made in Act I, i.e. twirling, leaning, playing a golf stroke, etc.*) It's a bit s-s-small, isn't it?
Alison It opens out, Burgess. Let me show you. (*She pulls it out, like a telescope, to its full size*)
Burgess So it does.
Alison *Now* you can lean on it.
Mabel Yes. (*He laughs and leans on it, then stares rather vaguely at Alison*)
Alison Or you can twirl it ... or—shelter under it ... or—anything ...
    What *is* it, Burgess? Don't you like the present I gave you?
Burgess Oh yes. Thank you, Alison. Only ...
Alison What?
Burgess There was something you said before you gave me the umbrella ...
Alison Yes?
Burgess I don't think I was listening properly ...
Alison I said I loved you.
Burgess Yes, I thought you did. Did you mean it?
Alison Of course. I've always loved you.

Burgess Really? Why, exactly?

Alison Because you're so clever and handsome and charming.

Burgess And you'd marry me?

Alison Tomorrow!

Burgess Then—*Alison* ...

Alison Yes?

Burgess I've made a startling discovery ...

Alison Yes?

Burgess I don't need an umbrella any more! (*He throws it away with abandon and falls on her neck*)

Alison Burgess! My beautiful present!

Burgess I don't need it. A man with a wife doesn't need an umbrella.

Alison Oh doesn't he?

Burgess *You'll* shelter me from the storm.

Alison Oh *yes*, Burgess!

Burgess I can lean on *you*.

Alison Oh *yes*, Burgess!

Song 20: The Umbrella Song (Reprise)

During this verse Burgess repeats some of his gestures from Act I, somewhat to Alison's alarm

Burgess   If you're a man of substance and you want it widely known
You must have a charming wife, for it can give a fellow tone
You can leave her in the office, if you're sure she won't be lost
For your colleagues to exclaim on her and what she must have cost
You can use her as a weapon if assaulted in the street
You can hide from any person whom you do not wish to meet,
You can stand and shake her, laughing, on the platform of a bus
You can whirl her, you can twirl her, you can lean upon her—thus!

They exit dancing to the tune of the Umbrella Chorus

As Burgess and Alison exit, Henrietta and Edward enter, dancing

Henrietta It's no good, Edward. I'm not in the mood for dancing.

Edward Nor I, really. In fact I think I'd better be going.

Henrietta Oh no Edward! Do stay. Have an ice-cream or something. I want you to stay.

Edward Why?

Henrietta Well—it's nice to have you at our party. We like you to be here. Besides—I told you—I've grown sort of—used to you.

Edward I'm no use here. I'll collect my costume and go.

Henrietta Edward ...

Edward I'm here under false pretences. Where's your aunt? I want to give her the money back. (*He feels in his pockets*) I've got some of it left and I'll give her an IOU for the rest. Abel!

Abel appears

My case, please. And my costume.

Abel exits

Henrietta Edward, I'm so sorry.
Edward What for? You can't help being in love with someone else.
Henrietta (*taking the bottle out of her bag, and moving downstage*)
No, I suppose I can't. You must think me very foolish and romantic.
Edward——

Abel enters with the case behind her

—I'm beginning to think so too. Of course the picture's all spoilt now——

Abel winks at Edward and goes

—but oh, if you could have seen him as he was once, in his prime—with
that beautiful beard——

Edward takes the beard out of case and puts it on

—And that wonderful rippling hair——

Edward puts on a rippling wig

—and that smile——

Edward smiles

—and that manly, vigorous look in his eyes——

Edward looks manly and vigorous

Oh Edward, if you could have seen him then——

*She turns and sees him. By now he is an exact replica of the advertisement
photograph. Henrietta screams*

Ah! It's him! It's Dr Beamish! No it's not. It's the model. The man I love.
No it's not. It's *you*, Edward!
Edward That's right, Henrietta. It's me.
Henrietta Oh take that horrible stuff off your face! I can't bear it. (*She
buries her face in her hands*)
Edward (*taking off the beard and wig*) Forgive me, Henrietta. I told you I
was here under false pretences. What made you buy that stupid tonic in
the first place?
Henrietta (*through tears*) I didn't buy it. It was in my s-s-stocking.
Edward (*snapping the case shut*) So it was all his doing. I might have known.
(*He goes to the door*) I'm sorry the end of your search was a disappointment, Henrietta. No, I'm worse than a disappointment, aren't I? I'm a
fake. But a fellow has to live. As you know I've been most things in my life
and modelling for Dr Beamish's "Moonshine" Elixir just happened to be
one of them. There's nothing in that tonic, you know. It's just coloured
water. How Uncle Charles got such a kick out of it, I can't imagine. And

how you ever fell in love with my photograph I can't imagine. Goodbye Henrietta.

Henrietta Edward, wait! There was a reason for what Father Christmas did. And there was a purpose to my search. But it wasn't to find the face in the photograph. It was to find what was behind it.

Edward And now that you have?

Henrietta I realize that what I wanted was here all the time.

Edward Henrietta . . .

Music. She goes to him and he takes her in his arms

He made us travel a long way, didn't he?

Song 20A: The Clue From the Cracker (Reprise)

Henrietta	How long ago our journey seems
Edward	We wandered through a world of dreams
	But they were real for this is true
	This joy I feel in finding you.

They kiss under the mistletoe and go

Excited entrance for all the Cousins

Rosie Surely it must be time for the presents!

Biddie I suppose he'll give them out himself.

Dora I'm longing for mine.

Edith Me too!

Eustace I hope I'll get some nice *big* ones.

Sidney The point is Eustace, have you *given* any nice big ones?

Eustace Good heavens, Sidney, of course not. I never do. Do you?

Sidney I should say not. No need to throw one's money around. That's not what Christmas is about.

Song 21: It's the Thought That Matters

The Cousins take up a close "choral" position and radiate piety. Eustace and Sidney lead the first verse, the Girls backing them with an "A-a-ah!"

Cousins When Christmastime is drawing near
We all get apprehensive
For Christmas shopping every year
Gets more and more expensive
But if your presents seem too small
Don't feel a guilt sensation
Just sing this Christmas madrigal
By way of consolation.

It's the thought that matters
Your relatives won't mind it
If the present is cheap
So long as you keep
An expensive thought behind it

It's the thought that matters
So keep your Christmas sunny
By giving your fill
Of love and goodwill
But not too much of your money.

Fa la la ... *etc.*

Solo lines What shall I get for Mother?
Nothing too pricey I hope.
She's sadly in need of a hairnet
And she'd welcome some carbolic soap.
She might like economy tissues,
Or something to keep the bath clean,
No, let's give the darling some glamour
I'll buy her a small tangerine!

What shall I get for Father?
Why not a lovely new pipe?
Something that's plain and not fancy
Yes, one of the bakelite type.
Or maybe a safety razor
With a packet of razor blades too,
That's far more than he ever gives me
Just the packet of blades will do!

Cousins It's the thought that matters
So when you're Christmas shopping
Don't worry at all that the present is small
If the thought behind is whopping
It's the thought that matters
Don't buy nice things just think 'em
It's easy to part with a gift of the heart
But it's hell to part with an income.

Fa la la ... *etc.*

Solo lines What shall I get for Clarice?
A bottle of cheap shampoo?
No, that's what you gave her last year
And her hair came out cornflower blue.
But you know that suspender she gave me
Well, now the elastic's gone slack
It isn't much use any longer
So why don't I give it her back?

What shall I get for Eric?
Something to deal with his skin?
No, that's a lost cause when you think
Of the state that his skin is now in.
He could have my old pair of cufflinks

Now that is a splendid idea
I could let him have one this Christmas
And give him the other next year
All It's the thought that matters
Rely on inspiration
And if you do your stuff
You can save up enough
For a winter sports vacation
It's the thought that matters
There's a message in these verses
And the truth it imparts
Is "open your hearts
And you need not open your purses."

Fa la la ... *etc.*

Music changes to the "Search" tune

Song 22: Finale

Abel, Disabel and Violet enter first, marshalling the Cousins into positions on either side of the stage. Then Charles and the three pairs of Lovers enter. Finally Father Christmas marches in, and during the following hands out presents from the tree

Father Christmas Now you've been a-hunting and you've shown a little sense
Everything's the same and yet you feel the difference
You've got what you were wanting and it's all the consequence
Of the search, search, search!
All You are the man
When all this began
Who drew up a plan
 Of the search.

You had in mind
The things we should find
And what lay behind
 The search, search, search, search.

You're the one who sent us up the hill and down the lane
Led us up the garden just to lead us back again
You are the one
Who had all the fun
Until we had done
 · The search, search, search
Until we had done.
 The search!

During the last note the telephone rings. While the music modulates, Mabel answers, then, after a pause:

Mabel (*speaking*)	Your reindeer said to ask you how long they have to wait
	They're feeling rather chilly and it's getting very late.
Father Christmas	They ought to be accustomed to waiting on the roofs
	If the silly things want warming they can go and boil their hoofs!

He laughs with childish glee at his witticism until he sees them all looking at him sternly

All (*singing*)   Don't be rude to a reindeer

When he's just a voice on a phone
If he's tethered out of earshot
Then he cannot hold his own
Jeering at a
Reindeer in his absence
Is a cowardly thing to do
You must never be rude to a reindeer
When he can't be rude to you.

Again the music modulates and Mabel speaks

Mabel	We'd like to give you something if you wouldn't think it strange
	So will you choose a present? It would make a little change.
Father Christmas	A present? How delightful! How magnificently new!
	I'll take this little lady—she will make me think of you.

He puts his arm round Violet

Violet	Then will I be a fairy? Ooh, thank you very much!
	At last I shall be Ultra, and have the magic touch!

Abel and Disabel join Father Christmas and Violet up C

Father Christmas	Goodbye! Goodbye!
All	Goodbye! Goodbye!
	We shall miss you.
Mabel	May I kiss you?
All	Come back next year!
Father Christmas	Yes, I'll be there
All	Just remember
	Next December!
Father Christmas	Next December
	I'll be there.

Father Christmas, Violet, Abel and Disabel exit up the chimney

All (*as they go*)   Drive with a care
                                We can none of us spare
                                You, so don't take a risk that is rash
                                We won't have you say
                                That you've broken your sleigh
                                In a slip, or a trip, or a crash!

                                At a breath-taking pace
                                They'll be flying through space
                                And be counting the mountains below
                                Oh if you're a stranger
                                You might think it dangerous
                                Seeing the speed that they—who-a!
                                Seeing the speed that they go.

*The sleigh-music dies away, the Lights fade very gradually, and the Guests
begin to depart*

1st Half   Good-night
Mabel *etc.*   You're going?
1st Half   We're going now, so thank you
Mabel *etc.*   Will you all be all right?
1st Half   Yes, the moon is bright
Mabel   A happy New Year!

1st Half exit

2nd Half   Good-night
Mabel *etc.*   You're going?
2nd Half   Oh thank you for the party
Mabel *etc.*   Mind how you go
                                In the frost and snow
All   A happy New Year!

2nd Half exit

Edward and Henrietta go off arm in arm the other way

*Left alone, Mabel blows out the candles on the tree one by one as the Chorus
off-stage quietly sing*

Chorus (*off*)   Candles at Christmastime
                                We bring them out at Christmastime
                                We light them every year
                                And as the flames appear
                                We feel the joy and cheer
                                Of Christmastime
                                Candles at Christmastime
                                But there's an end to Christmastime
                                And when it passes by
                                We snuff them with a sigh

And so we say goodbye
To Christmastime.

The last candle is out. Mabel goes

Only the glow of the fire is left

CURTAIN

Curtain Call

All   Christmastime's a merry time
And he the great big world will span
To make the world a merry world
For he's a merry gentleman
   Heigh-ho! The holly berry
   May your Christmases be merry
   May your peace and comfort grow
   Underneath the mistletoe
Christmastime's a merry time
And he does all that Christmas can
To make the world a merry world
For he's a merry gentleman
He's a merry
Very, very merry
Merry, Merry, Merry, Merry
Gentleman
A merry gentleman
A merry, merry, merry, merry
Gentleman
A very merry
Gentleman.

FURNITURE AND PROPERTY LIST

ACT I

On stage: Settee
Armchair
Large fireplace. *In it:* fire, telephone
Christmas tree. *On it:* decorations, candle lights, presents, suitable props for Song 18 (Act III) e.g. hats, musical instruments. *Behind it:* sack of presents
Giant cracker. *In it:* clues
Mistletoe

Off stage: Lighted taper **(Mabel)**
Trays of drinks **(Abel, Disabel, Violet)**
Umbrella **(Burgess)**
Small suitcase containing Father Christmas outfit **(Charles)**
Several umbrellas **(Disabel)**
Umbrellas **(Eustace, Sidney)**
Small present **(Mabel)**
Bag of clues on salver **(Abel)**
Bag of clues on salver **(Disabel)**
Handbag containing wand **(Violet)**

Personal: **Henrietta:** handbag containing bottle with photograph

During transformation on page 26, bring on sleigh

ACT II

On stage: Fir-trees
2 reindeer heads on either side of door to Father Christmas's Winter Palace

Off stage: Miniature sleigh **(Charles)**
Clues **(Abel, Violet)**
Clues **(Company)**
Umbrella, clue **(Burgess)**
Clue **(Alison)**
Clue **(Henrietta)**
Clue **(Mr Ough)**
Blow-up of "Moonshine" advertisement **(Abel** and **Disabel,** or **Father Christmas)**
Signpost **(Abel)**
Chemical contraption **(Mabel** and **Violet)**
Clue on salver **(Abel)**
Bouquet **(Father Christmas)**
Clue **(Henrietta)**

Clue **(Edward)**
Clue **(Burgess)**
Burgess's umbrella **(Alison)**
Clue **(Mr Ough)**
Bottle **(Rosie)**
Book of Spells **(Mabel)**
Hat, cloak **(Violet)**

Personal: **Snowman:** hat, pipe
Girls: muffs
Mabel: wand
Henrietta: handbag with bottle, handkerchief
Alison: handbag with locket

ACT III

On stage: As Act I

Set: Giant cracker open
Clues strewn over floor
Wrapped telescopic umbrella behind tree

Off stage: Trays of drinks **(Abel** and **Disabel)**
Case containing beard and wig **(Abel)**

Personal: **Henrietta:** handbag with bottle

LIGHTING PLOT

Property fittings required: fire effect, candle lights on Christmas tree

A drawing-room, the roof-tops, Christmasland

ACT I. Evening

To open: Fire effect on

Cue 1	During **Song 1** *Bring up candle lights on tree as* **Mabel** *lights them; gradually bring up general interior lighting*	(Page 1)
Cue 2	During 2nd refrain of **Song 5** *Subtle lighting change as* **Father Christmas** *comes down chimney—fade fire effect until he is on stage*	(Page 16)
Cue 3	**Father Christmas:** "SILENCE!!" *Flicker lights; snap on and off fire effect*	(Page 17)
Cue 4	**Father Christmas** does his Magic Gesture *Snap off fire effect*	(Page 18)
Cue 5	**Mabel** gestures at fire *Snap on fire effect*	(Page 20)
Cue 6	**Father Christmas:** "Magic Work, Begin the Game." *Change lights*	(Page 25)
Cue 7	During **Song 7** *Change lights with music; fade fire effect*	(Page 26)
Cue 8	**Alison** quietly begins to sing *Bring up spot on* **Alison**	(Page 26)
Cue 9	**Henrietta** repeats refrain with **Alison** *Bring up spot on* **Henrietta**	(Page 26)
Cue 10	**Henrietta, Alison, Mabel** and **Father Christmas** exit up chimney *Change lighting as scene transforms to roof-tops—concentrate lighting on sleigh*	(Page 26)

ACT II.

To open: Sparkling exterior lighting

Cue 11	**Mabel** makes a third Gesture *Dramatic lighting change*	(Page 53)
Cue 12	**Mabel:** "Down to Earth, and Home you go!" *Sudden lighting change—bright, sparkling lighting*	(Page 55)

ACT III.   Evening

To open: General interior lighting, tree candle lights on, fire effect on

Cue 13   **Mabel:** "... pretend nothing happened."   (Page 58)
            Change lights; fire effect off

Cue 14   Sleigh-music dies away   (Page 71)
            Fade lights gradually; bring up fire effect

Cue 15   **Mabel** blows out candles on tree   (Page 71)
            Snap off candle lights as she does so

EFFECTS PLOT

ACT I

Cue 1	**Henrietta:** "Of course. This way." *Doorbell rings*	(Page 12)
Cue 2	**Henrietta** exits with **Edward** *Doorbell rings*	(Page 12)
Cue 3	**Mr Ough:** "No idea." *Doorbell rings*	(Page 13)
Cue 4	**Father Christmas:** "Help the seekers to find the way." *Bags of clues flash or jump*	(Page 24)
Cue 5	**Mabel:** "You're wonderful!" *Telephone rings*	(Page 24)
Cue 6	**Father Christmas:** "Magic Work, Begin the Game." *Smoke rises from giant cracker*	(Page 25)

ACT II

Cue 7	**Charles:** "Listen." *Sleigh bells off*	(Page 31)
Cue 8	**Mabel:** "... he's angry with me. No wonder!" *Snow effect*	(Page 53)

ACT III

Cue 9	**Mr Ough:** "... not sure I ever lost it." *Telephone rings*	(Page 58)
Cue 10	**All** (*singing*): "The search!" *Telephone rings*	(Page 69)

MADE AND PRINTED IN GREAT BRITAIN BY
LATIMER TREND & COMPANY LTD, PLYMOUTH
MADE IN ENGLAND